COVID DIARY

Verse for Survivors

by

Victoria Floor

OTHER BOOKS BY VICTORIA FLOOR

Via Terra

Dee Generation

80% Cacao

Trouble With Poets

Crone-icles

Mutter, Falter

Just a Song at Twilight

Permaculture

I'll Ask 'Er

My Sweet, Short Death

2018: Ms. America's Bad Case of the Trumps

Artana

Biking in the Wind

Brandish: The Dominatrix of Silver Spring

ISBN: 9798593103765

For C, the Constant...

"History doesn't repeat itself
[thank gods!] but it often rhymes."

—Samuel Clemens

INTRODUCTION:
I live in Princeton, New Jersey, a lovely college town surrounded by rolling farm country, with houses dating back to the early 18th century.   I can walk and/or bike to all stores and services and have plenty access to woods and fields. (Princeton is still less crowded than most parts of New Jersey.)
When Covid hit here, I didn't have much of an adjustment to make in my daily routines, as I live alone and am retired. The thought of isolating was hardly a challenge. However, in December 2019, I had been hired to work the tourist season in a store in Rocky Mountain National Park, beginning early May. Because of (and thanks to) new Covid social distancing requirements, the job started a month later, and resulted in each crew member having a private room—ah, privacy! I was worried about traveling and about working indoors, but took the risk, and so spent from early June through mid-October in Western mountain splendor. What follows reflects both settings: Princeton and Colorado. There are also a few entries written in Maryland and Vermont during brief escapes across state lines.
Beginning in mid-March of 2020, I'd decided to keep a journal on the essence of each day, or the things I was thinking of when I settled down to write, usually in the evening just before bed.   As much as the rampant pandemic, the U.S. political crises were galloping and dramatic—I could not have ignored them if I'd tried.

You may envision a white woman with shoulder-length white-blond hair, sitting at her laptop, often with a smile on her face. She has survived this challenging year by enjoying Nature's bounty, talking and texting daily with loved ones, trysting with her lover, and regularly meeting with various groups via the internet platform, Zoom. She listened to her favorite pundits and commentators, read inspiring books, watched illuminating documentaries, as well as purely entertaining TV. In short, she had a normal and pleasant time of it, particularly because she has not (as of this writing) suffered a personal loss due to Covid.

She is forever grateful for her health and to all the good people who help keep her sane. You may be one of them...if so, her deepest thanks!

—Victoria Floor

Princeton, NJ

January 2021

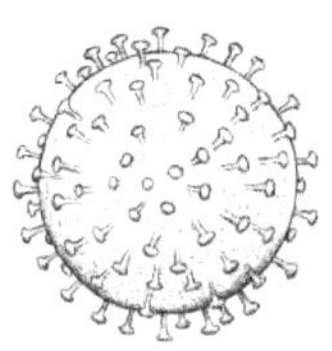

Mar 15, 2020 (The Ides)
My Daughter's Stuck in France at Her Sibling's
Place Due to Covid Flight Restrictions

Today my baby girl turned 33
and in her honor, (or perhaps, her memory),
well spread-apart in freshest air,
I planted jonquils in the woods in sun
with several neighbors, then hiked a bit
and looked in vernal pools for globs of eggs
of salamanders, frogs—I here report:
that though my daughter's far away in France,
her brother made her treats and has a Parisienne
who helped him cook this birthday feast,
shared with me in picture and in text.
And lo, indeed, the vernal pools held life:
amphibious and otherwise, as true
as bulbs beneath the soil will sprout, without
us here to witness or to shout about.

Mar 16
Random Act of Kindness

I biked along the old Millstone canal
and saw the turtles out without the sun,

March wind normal as the buds were red,
while talking to my friend in Maryland,
the phone jammed in my helmet, freeing hands
with which I took up pebbles to be tossed
into the lake from the bridge back home.
'Twas there I saw a billfold on the path —
a man's it was; I rode to leave a note
to stick in his front door, then called the cops,
who found his number. Soon he called to say
he'd bike to me from where he'd gone to look,
retracing steps the way we write our lives...
He seemed so happy, all it took to say:
"We don't need more to panic at today..."

Mar 17

Self-portrait on Day of Her Birth

This day, Mom's victory — her first-born kid —
did walk an easy mile to store and back
accompanied by neighbor friend and chat;
she bought herself some birthday treats and sat
a-bench, savoring the company a bit.
Then home, alone, in quarantine again,
placed her new pink hyacinths in light,
devoured chocolate as she whiled away
the bleak remains of this St. Patrick's day,
reminded how, once more, all life is cheap,
while death stalks human bunnies as a fox
and no more precious present shall she keep
than white strands glinting through her fading
locks.

Mar 18
Lifelines

Another day passed tethered to the line:
the one we spent our youth on with a cord,
cordless, now, but just as sweet, divine.
The sound of loved-ones' voices hovered near
like falcons soaring over huts and caves
connecting souls across the ragged lands,
a satellite threading us by gaze,
distraction from the news that fills our days
and keeps us tenter-hooked and asking when
we might embrace our loved ones once again.

Mar 19
Secret Joys

Is it evil to be happy in these times?
Having relaxed with friends in phone visits,
biked to the store,
baked healthy cookies with chocolate chips,
walked with my neighbor,
started a 2,000 piece puzzle of San Francisco,
read prose and poetry well-crafted,
caught up on the news,
exchanged texts with my lancer,
washed and replaced clothes and linens,
checked in with my kids in France and my ex- in
Mexico,
gotten in bed with a full stomach, chuckling at
the exposure

of corrupt politicians by courageous journalists,
feeling no more guilt for exempting self
from acts of kindness and generosity
to take care of me, myself and I,
to romp and play
in beloved solitude.

I grieve not for my virulent species.
No end in sight, but certainly
a new beginning:
Spring is just —
well, springing!

Mar 20
Never for The Last Time

Because it was going to be seventy,
(not an old day, but a warm one),
I set off for the beach,
(not for the last time, as DS would say:
"I'm going riding for the last time,
I'm going skiing for the last time,"
because I don't yet know that I'm dying
and so far, so not sick,
so maybe I'll be back to revisit)
dunes where blond foxes nap, and where,
this time, I retraced my steps
following my own footprints,
to see if I could find the socks fallen
from the side pocket of my backpack
where I'd stuffed a bunch of dead balloons
destined to destroy sealife.

As we celebrate ourselves into our graves,
as DS did, I will, as the species must
if it's to survive itself
through the bottleneck devolving,
retrace steps
to when we were small
in number and in brain,
relatively harmless
like the sun today.
Though the sunscreen did nothing
but sting my eyes
and the wind worked at me
as it sculpts an old log,
it felt so good to go sockless
in rubber shoes
that let the March sea in
to anoint my toes.

(I never did find those socks.)

Mar 21
Earth's Great Composers

Ulsula K. Leguin writes
of John Luther Adams,
who played us the Earth
in Fairbanks, Alaska,
which I'd heard in July of
'17 when I'd needed
reminding that Mother
will sing to Her children
songs dreadful and brilliant

as weather, as mountains,
volcanoes and icebergs.
She never stops wailing,
that Banshee of Banshees,
our one-breasted planet
where all of us riders
asleep in our saddles
are mixing our poisons
deep in Her cauldrons,
forsaken, frostbitten
and boiled to extinction,
with Ulsula watching
as John Luther takes her
on magical starships
to her own private Heaven.

And I down this day here
writing and speaking,
as if on a mission
to spin out more truth-tales,
remembering language
in all of its stories.

Mar 22
What to Talk About?

Communion continues with family and friends,
plague is tenacious,
news never ends...

What of the workers?
How will they get paid?

What of TP hoarders?
Could there be a raid
conducted at gunpoint
by armed paranoics?
What of the firemen
policemen and medics?
WWIII's been declared,
who now shall lead us?
Capitalist piggies
are still gonna bleed us
(though someday their robots
will probably need us).

Mar 23
Searching for Meaning

I'd said I'd find some yoga on the net,
then lost to my fat, lazy self that bet
and let the rainy day dictate the stuff
I chose to do, deciding 'twas enough.
I'm making progress on that puzzle and
writing missives to some thoughtful friends,
while chatting long and late in every style
of conversation, 'til the chit-chat ends
in near exhaustion from such social ties
as I would not indulge in normal times,
but we must now endeavor to ensure
each loved one that we're here and that we're
sure
we'll be among the blessed ones that pull
through—
of course we will—and more than I and you

will live way past this round until we learn
surviving is a thing we have to earn
as viruses 2, 3, to 85, attack in sequence,
neither dead nor live,
mysterious and stealthy as they are,
aliens from some fantastic star
and yet no one among us wants to give
up something so another one might live
as selfishness is really what you need
if you're to make it—this is what I read
in books like Frankl's which make rather clear:
heroics have no place, while measured fear
is what should drive one past catastrophe.
I want my tribe to be as wise as he.

Mar 24
Just Past Equinox

How slow time hobbles when the future's
blocked
with all the treasure chests and coffers locked.
The birds sing louder as the world is hushed.
The pace is slowed, though bicycles are rushed
past strollers as the biker holds her breath—
as if this somehow shields her from mere death.
As life's returning, snakes out in the grass,
turtles sunning, flowers now outclass
the forests lagging just a bit behind
in shadow still, as if a peace of mind
was cooling as the sun shines ever bright
upon each day as long as any night.
For dreaming souls now twisting in suspense

as looming flashes making little sense
deliver news devoid of clarity
as muddy as the rain-soaked path. You see,
we sleep now with a wary open eye
upon the groaning orb that scuttles by.

Mar 25
Nightmare Shared

Some sleep long and deep,
escaping from the light;
others vigils keep,
focus all their might.
But waking from this dream
all gasp, remembering
nothing now is real...
the day no light can bring,
no warm companion feel.
Nightmare it may seem —
alarm bell yet to ring.

Mar 26
Sniffing Daffodils While the World Reels

With peak of Spring now underway,
on the evening news they say
we've got more cases here than there,
(though soon we'll see it everywhere).
When Africa goes down in turn
I wonder what this world will learn.

Is humility in play?
Or will we merely end this way?
If wars break out with plague, it seems
no youngster shall live out her dreams
and that would be okay with me,
though sad to have to lose TV,
where droning pundits bathe our brains
'til little intellect remains
with which, best case, we could adapt,
but humans seem to be more apt
to let the endtimes roll on by...
Save lives? Who'd even care to try?
I'd rather bike and walk around,
smelling blossoms on the ground,
kneeling down as if in prayer,
a singing robin, unaware.

Mar 27
Recording Most Foul

So Dylan's going out in hail of song.
I hope he doesn't think there's something wrong
with building monuments or writing notes.
(I'm more concerned that each survivor votes
and gets us past this piss-poor president,
on to the biz for which our world is meant;
that is, reforming humans best we can,
each living woman, enby, child, and man.)
We need to hang on long enough to see
if one can transmute to one's own pc,
if ghosts in shells will roam this planet still
behaving like us, though without ill will...

I think in Dylan's way he's said it all:
our world, like JFK's, is bound to fall.
Since all who die of aging simply miss
their children's innovations — think of this:
the infants born today will live to see
a different flavor of humanity
and still consider our times as they need.
For some of history is bound to seed
ideas that never blossomed in their time,
but wait, like flowers, for a warmer clime.
And warmer it shall be, at least awhile...
Will Dylan and his set go in their file
in case youth needs to hear that raspy voice?
Remember: their survival's still *their* choice.

Mar 28
Local Drama

This morning woke me at the dawn:
outside my bedroom, on the lawn
a fox was screaming at wits end,
I guessed in order to defend
her kits from one great big raccoon.
I watched them, clear as if at noon,
a mere four feet from where I stood
with window glass between — and good
feelings flooded me just then,
imagining the fox's den
was just behind me in the park.
I'll listen for the parents' bark
and hope to see their kits one day
and to my mother's ghost I say:

"Thanks for checking in on me
eternal vixen, Fox Lady.
I'm fine and so are your grand-kits
and all the love that in us fits
into this day we'll all see through
and think of all our ghosts, for you
are also in a good place now,
safe, protected, yet somehow
engaged as we are with this time,
so close to yours, yet now sublime.
You watch as through a window here:
fierce protectors, keeping clear
the dens we dwell in, rain or shine."

For you I make this Valentine.

Mar 29

An Upside of Covid

Satellites agree: the view from space
confirms our sphere's indeed a cleaner place
since planes have grounded, traffic ceased to
flow,
buildings closed and most folks moving slow,
as if slow-motion softens brutal scenes
or helps our eyes decide what action means
when following a butterfly in flight
whose motion through the atmosphere just
might
produce another outcome — wait and see...
Now several thousands satellites agree:

the Earth is smiling through her dirty face
upon a virus as an act of grace.

Mar 30
Poisoned Reflecting Pools

I threw away the faded flowers,
too much mirror; now my wrinkles
chastise louder, waking hours
mostly prostrate, Rip Van Winkles...
not the beauty in glass coffin.
Biking off to get fresh jonquils
from the woods where once Narcissus
tortured Echo with his mirror
always fretting over beauty
never seeing beauty really.
Why are faded flowers ugly?

Today was sadder, grayer, lonely;
today was also restful, hopeful.
Could the panic soon be peaking?
Will the wreckage leave us seeking
better leaders, better vision
fresher, younger, brighter? Or will
the young ones age now sadly
banished Echos, lost, forgotten?
Will there be another future?
Or will all this end in torture?
If oppression gets much stronger,
workers won't exist much longer.
Let the moguls in their manholes
cringe beneath the fading forests

like Narcissus, futures frozen.
Then our younger ones can leave them,
make a world of wild new gardens.
As my flesh and muscle hardens,
as I fade, and rightly so,
I'll call my name, then let me go.

Mar 31
How to Shoprite

Today I took the plunge and shopped for food.
I'd made my larder last a safe long time,
but now it seemed appropriate and good
to don bandanna — not to commit a crime,
but cover face to keep my hands away
and think of social distance in each aisle.
It took an hour, then I had to pay,
touch surfaces, I, too would thus defile.
Once safe at home, I'd sanitize the lot,
scrubbing all with soap and watered bleach.
Of course there was a washing I forgot
— though tub, shampoo and soap in easy reach.
I didn't strip and shower right away,
which I may live to rue another day.
So far, my sense of smell and taste seem fine
and nothing feels awry in nose or throat.
I'm not the type to worry or to whine,
but rather one to write myself a note:
"To all who care, I took a risk today
and entered Covid germ-infested store
to try to take another month to play
this game of 'Am I clean? I can't be sure'..."

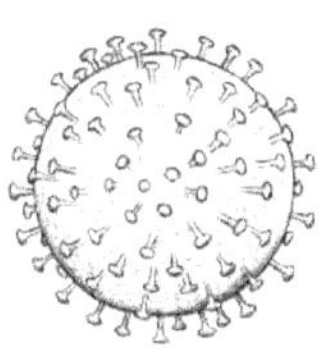

Apr 1
"Only Connect"

O artists! It's our duty to create,
to save mankind with sensibility,
and yet it now appears a trifle late
to thus respond to this fresh tragedy,
while witnessing more death than ever seen
crack amongst us sudden as a storm.
I wonder if my wit is now less keen,
while bodies from this morning are still warm
and no one knows if such a nightmare ends,
or if we've met our fate from here on out.
The artist offers hope and thus pretends
that faith can wield a pen to banish doubt.
If art could save us now we'd all emote;
more eloquent our requiems would be.
Today there's something stuck in every throat
depriving seers of the eyes to see
around a corner longer than a war
and sink us deeper than the murky sea.
For rhymes, like merry dance, are growing sore.
The tarantella, frantically we do.
My poet's voice can't sing, nor even shout
above the sirens' harsh hullabaloo
to tell the future what now's all about.
When artists fail it means there's only dust,

like rusty water coming from the tap.
I took a tainted bath tonight; I trust
I'm now prepared to take a lonely nap
and give to dreams what can't be written here:
we're all to sleep through silent spring this year.

Apr 2
Eat the Rich

Caligula now rules the ol' U.S.
and leaves us in an ever-growing mess,
securing for his family its wealth,
while sacrificing every worker's health.
I spend the day attempting to do some
small offices to help them not succumb
to poverty and sickness as they will,
for *this*, my countrymen's, a bitter pill.

Though trees and flowers bloom unto their peak,
it's been a most distressing plague-filled week,
yet I'm most comforted to find a friend
has chosen to communicate again,
while one old boyfriend sends a sloppy verse
entitled "April's Cruelest Month" — and worse,
describes his life of luxury as though
he's taking comfort in a pile of dough.
Yet signs of revolution fill the air
and workers dare to strike in places where
a while ago they never would have dared
(for no one 'til this moment could have cared
if leveling of classes could ensue).
I hope each wealthy asshole gets his due.

Ex-lovers and ex-presidents alike...
Caligulas — beware May's lightning strike!

Apr 3
We're All Outlaws Now

Another day, bandannas in the street
covering the face as to defeat
the notion that a friendly shake or hug
would not invite the rampant deadly bug.
I wore my kerchief to the local bank.
If only I'd a pistol I might rank
among the wildwest heroes of the day
when some rebellious dudes could get away
with taking money from the rich to give
to poor folk who might otherwise not live,
(a thought so foreign to our class today).
It seems the virus ought to sweep away
the crumbs of evil aristocracy,
the kleptocrats that steal democracy,
bandannaless, no pistol in their belt,
but with a hand of cards they'd once been dealt
by Lady Fortune, who may flee them now,
for She is needed elsewhere. And I vow
to join the looters when they storm the stores
as long as such a just revolt endures...

Apr 4

Waiting to Hear About Job in Rocky Mountains

A day of stolen daffodils and peeks
at newscasts that haven't changed in weeks,
except to tell us numbers growing fast!
I wish I'd hear the number of days passed
in quarantine would be outnumbered soon
and healthy days would steadily balloon
and I could spend the summer far away
in mountains where my heart so yearns to play.
I cross my fingers daily that I will,
but there will be at least another hill
as Covid charts it curvy-headed course,
not flat enough to undermine its source.
Though vaccines in production may prove good
and wearing masks is what all say we should
be doing, all except the president,
who wouldn't sacrifice a single cent
of his fake fortune for N95s
to save our workers busy saving lives.

This day was lovely—walk and ride in woods,
stealing jonquils, sharing stolen goods
with neighbors and with family, for whom,
I await tomorrow's visits via Zoom...

Apr 5
Remembering Dear DS

You barged into my morning thoughts, a fist:
of course—it's your birthday! You would have been
sixty-nine today and I would say to you:

"A guy only turns sixty-nine once—
that's a big deal!
We must celebrate!" remembering how you
took me six years ago to whoop it up
in fancy DC restaurant with all
my local family 'round,
even my dad, who, like you,
escaped Trump Era and its plagues,
escaped recession woes, yet worse,
and all the aches and pains of aging more
and further degradation of our slopes,
where snow you'd loved would now be banished
and riding trails so muddy you might fall
and hurt your back again and never heal...
So glad you didn't have to feel
the horror of autocracy descend,
your beloved Congress choked, inept,
and even going to the polls unsure,
as rituals and rites that gave us hope
peel away, placentas from retriever pups...
I'm looking out for fox kits in my park
and promise I will share this joy with you
should little yelps and yips disclose their den;
and I'll commune with you precisely when

the moon is bright, or dark reveals your star;
for wherever I am still is where you are.

Apr 6
"When the Truth Offends We Lie"

I'm studying the decline and fall of civilizations,
just to prep.
The miniseries "Chernobyl" predicates the
Soviet collapse — a short-lived
empire indeed! But then the other miniseries
"Roman Empire" sends
shivers of recognition — they'd had it all:
environmental degradation, including self-
poisonings through lead,
corrupt and degenerate leadership,
nepotism and kleptocracy,
entrenched oligarchs that controlled the
executive
and boy, did they have plagues!
Extreme economic inequality, oppressed
peoples, oppressed women, oppressed animals:
oppression ruined Rome and ruins us.

The weight of uranium, the weight of lead, the
oppressive smog of coal and the heaviness
of news ever shriller yet ever duller, its total
impact oppressive to the wary citizens
for, as with each empire before ours, the sacred
bonds
of trust between plebes and government
(no matter what style of government)

once broken, are not repaired...
Our crumbling empire's fall brings so much
grief,
I cut my hair — in truth, there's no relief.

Apr 7
A Whale of a Silence

Let me sing my spring song,
for once you may hear:
whales and their birds rejoicing
from seas somewhat hushed
under mild northern skies
where the pink moon presides,
great blossom to signal
her reign of indifference.
For after their death knells
we savor the silence,
their churches as empty
as the land 'round Chernobyl.
Now the name of a right whale
is sung to the heavens
and all who can hear him
will light up with moonglow
and all who can see him
will believe in their future.

I listened to music
of 1971 from a
show then recorded
and heard in one song
the line: "If you live to

2005..." — well we have,
some of us, and
may still be alive.

Apr 8

Desperately Reading Whitehead

When Einstein re-described the world,
Whitehead tried to then apply
relativity to *us* — that is
the living, not the void —
to re-describe without such words
as "ecosystem" or "chaos theory,"
nor "multiverse." (For those Als? No sirs!)
Instead he used the concept "God"
(for which Whitehead lowercases "he"):
that strange force — we now call "weak"
that somehow drives the dance and I,
looking back a century at greater minds
wrestling with such visions to articulate,
am humbled as I now bike past
the building where dear Albert parked
his bike and tried and tried
(until that great Jew up and died)
to go beyond his younger work,
to take us farther than the gods,
to build Olympus new from scratch...
His failure humbled him, I'm sure,
and now in Princeton there's a store
that sells his image as a saint;
(Albert surely said he ain't).
We worship science — I know *I* do —

while never knowing what is true.
So maybe lies, like Trump's, aren't bad;
in another universe they might
tell us truths? Today it's sad
to face another peak of death
statistics in my region, though
I try to dwell in love and light,
the thunder woke me, and I know
Whitehead smiles upon us all.

It feels so good to be so small.

(Methinks the "God" force of last century
now bears the holy name: "Dark Energy.")

Apr 9
Ode to the Season

You are more beautiful than the most exquisite
maiden.
Your new grass is greener than her emerald
eyes,
your spring clouds soft and plumper than her
young breasts,
your springs, sweet and fresher than her wet
kisses,
your wind-sculpted sands smoother than her
belly,
your sunlight skies bluer than the veins in her
temples,
your blossoming tulips, red, redder than her full
lips,

your tangling vines than her curling locks,
your birds' chatter than her conversing,
your lion's moan than she comes her sex,
your great mountains stand prouder than her
bold buttocks,
your moths flutter faster than her hands at work,
your breezes blow sweeter than her singing
breath,
your rain falls warmer than her tears of joy,
as she beholds you —
in a stepmother's mirror —
for You are fairest of them all!
You, not she, for she is but a fragment
and You, *You* are the *World*!

Apr 10

Did He Say "Blessed Are the Cheesemakers"?

"So fuck the meek!" my sister used to jest,
and now, the Bible's failed the Jesus test:
the meek have fallen for the rest of us.
It's clear nobody's gonna make a fuss
as paupers fill the pits prepared for men
who'll never get a chance, not even when
the rich could buy them all a thousand years...
but now is not a time to shed those tears.
For if the meek do rise it won't take long
to still the rich and sing a new day's song.
Out on old streets the hungry young will throng
while meeks around the world will sing along...

Apr 11
Self-indolent

Alas, the day hath come when even I
did while away the hours zoning out,
allowing every neural cell to fly
until by nightfall there remained no doubt
I'd chosen to annihilate all thought,
whilst all around emergency's declared,
for many of my neighbors now have caught
the virus, though I have merely dared
to take a walk with weights, then eat and watch
a marathon soap-opera on the tube,
knowing all the while I'd surely scotch
all true creative output, like a rube,
consuming numbing pap to soothe my soul;
I gulped an old HBO miniseries whole!

Apr 12
Pasquale Hope for Advances Come of Covid

Easter Sunday and the air is clear:
resuscitation, resurrection-style.
It would be quite amazing if this fear
results in cleaner heavens for awhile:
to see the stars at night, remember how
the world was once, not many moons ago,
to see ourselves as hapless infants now
and not the masters of a world of woe
where waters *must* be darkened,
skies *must* gray,
where everything *has to* wither and decay...

If we had harkened to our Mother's voice
we'd see such suffering was but our choice,
and just because our infant greed grew strong,
we didn't have to wallow in it long,
but *could*, like Jesus, come again to life
and *could*, by virtue over greed, end strife.
For, species long oppressed by human need
to conquer every surface and to breed
beyond our Mother's milk supply to nurse
so many babies—now live out the curse
humanity had put upon Her soil,
and from now on, commit ourselves to toil
to keep those skies fresh as they are right now
and find a way back to Her womb, somehow...

Apr 13
As Ends the Rain

A day of rainy news and cooking fires,
agonies and pleasantries alike—
as stark as life can be without a war.
A war is worse. Of this, at least, I'm sure.
The rain did end and out we walked well-
masked,
my neighbor friend and I, a lonesome pair
of single gals united once a day
for exercise—a grownup form of play.
I stole some blossoms as I headed home,
the grass as emerald as its icon says,
and ate the treats I'd cooked, then took a bath...
Life sure is good—so far—and I'm so glad,
I'm glad, I'm glad, I'm glad to hear the birds

returned from under bushes to their limbs;
I'm sad, I'm sad, I'm sad, I'm not with him,
my lancer; missing him is now required.

Apr 14
Busy Beeing in Twisted Time

While consuming news I use my hands.
Jigsaw puzzles work quite well.
Today I cut up magazines,
a collage to craft — it came out swell!
My friend's crocheting coasters now,
another's sewing masks for docs.
The days roll by like cattle trains.
By the hour we check our clocks.
When bedtime comes we wonder, "Say,
it's Monday, right? Or perhaps Tuesday?"
The endless quarantine is fraught
with novel pains: should I have bought
more medicines and food supplies?
I now go walking in disguise
which never bothers me — it ought?

"Now is the time that tries men's souls"
(if by "now" was meant more than black holes).

Apr 15
Wounded Raven

No one I know has died of this
new virus so mysterious

and mute.
Its silence brings us birdsong,
yet no magic flute
can overcome
the demon's deadly hiss...
I cower in my cavern, not to cry
for souls in flight from panic in the streets,
as empire dies before us, though we try
to live.
The one "disease" our government defeats
is justice, now just a
wounded raven
limping by.

Apr 16
Zola Day

Don stockpiled ventilators; shipped to Vlad.
His minions take to streets—they're piping mad.
They can't abide the rules to stay housebound.
(They won't be missed when Covid mows them
down.)

In the bloody riot scene in *Germinal*
the miners rise and capture someone rich
and rip his balls off, carry on a stick
the flabby manhood, symbol of the damned.
And yet the proles can never rule for long;
the rich return like fleas upon the hound,
and no one dares to scratch the loathsome itch
for fear that cur will bite us on the fist
we raise against the bourgeois tyrant, deaf

to all the clamoring he cowers from...
So now we gather balls of oligarchs
and hope the storied day, like summer, comes.

Apr 17
Noted

Some, when sick, are writing final notes
to loved ones, just in case
we never get to meet more face-to-face.
We're hoarding love, for love
is all we can send in the end.
And maybe love will prove a better friend
when but a thread to tie us to this world
until into the void our selves are hurled.
And maybe those who lost us when
will read our notes and thank us then.

Apr 18
Release the Doves!

The War on Death is raging still
and yet our lords would move to kill
the peace that keeps us safe inside;
white monsters take to streets and chide
the science that we've come to love,
while I feed breadcrumbs to a dove
and watch my far-flung son rehearse
the moves that might remove this curse.
While hope is called a tepid thing,

all around the bells won't ring.
Now they ring both day and night.
(I'd rather watch the doves in flight.)

Apr 19
Daffodils Displaced

Today as some reflected on those killed
a quarter century ago and thus fulfilled
mad-whitemen dreams of terrorism here,
I wandered in the woodlands free of fear,
examining the life that neither billed
nor willed itself to be. Or so suggests
Whitehead, who describes a drawing near
toward pleasures of all kinds, eschewing fear,
to curdle into forms, some animate,
others just as quiet as the stone...
Some stones explode in frost and never wait
to travel through erosion nor to hone
their essences. The daffodils' estate
I moved from over here to over there,
plants animated way beyond their wills.
Though one might argue they were free from care,
I'm sure they felt the rumblings of the earth
as if explosions wracked their settled place,
shook fragile stems and bulbs for all they're worth.
These transplants should survive, assuming grace.

Apr 20

A Succulent Berry

Time passes slowly in the sad times of Covid;
we don't have a Shelley, no Shakespeare, no Ovid,
we've lost Rachel Carson and old Robert Frost,
but there's one Nature poet, we still haven't lost:
O Wendell, O Wendell, you're a young eighty-five!
So glad at this moment you're more than alive.
I know you'll go down as the bard of these times
and forgive me my doggerel, second-grade rhymes,
but I love how you tell it in sonorous tones,
that Nature is wiser than all our smart phones,
that She knows what she's doing and does it so well,
that the path we're pursuing will lead us to Hell
and the moral be told by some creature with gills...
There are too many species to go down with our ills,
that our suffering suits us, it's merely our shroud,
this wonderful weapon She's thrown at our crowd
as we storm through Her barricades, spoiling for fight,
as She creams us with arrows then bids us good-night.
O Wendell you know how I feel for this day,

that the Great Times have come and it's my turn
to say:
I have never loved my kind as much as I should,
while I've longed for a Kind Mind to do us some
good,
as only our Mother who holds us up high
to admire a blossom against a blue sky.
You point us to Mother like every good son.
O Wendell, I thank you! Your work's almost
done.

Apr 21
Breechbirths and Walks With Fitbits

Nothing so delicious as biking home just before
the big thunderstorm hits.
My little burrow is my own; I fit it as well as the
fox fits
its den and here I nurse myself as it would nurse
its new kits.
A baby born to our extended family today elicits
more joys as life irrepressible makes ever more
bits
of flesh from flesh through transforming old
tidbits,
though we may not be the best form that now
sits
enthroned upon the planet throwing wild fits.
An infant bawling as its head hits
the cradle board — it pisses and shits
upon itself, its little balled mitts
pound the cradle as parental nitwits

no longer know how to evade pits
of their despair at losing their wits.
If nothing consumed can fill the mess kits,
we sit and stare as this passing storm spits
a few last drops before the rain quits...
I hope we're not just human dipshits
about to call our short-lived reign quits,

Apr22
BEarthday

Fifty years ago, a teenaged girl.
sat on the lawn of Fairmount Park
listening to speeches by the likes of
Ed Muskie and Allen Ginsberg...
She could not have conjured
a corona pandemic
and a landscape more peaceful
and air more clear
and streets more silent
than this Earth Day
of her dotage.
While her once young hope wanes
for future dreams,
as the curse of course correction
descends to settle scores
and set straight some very
broken bones of democracy,
while whales suckle their young
on one coast and starve on another,
while we know we were laggards,
we could have come early

to that very first Earth Day:
her coming-out party.

Apr 23
Gifted

This day brought the vulture pair
nesting again in the loft
of the old corn crib by the red barn
where we cut brush in our masks,
social-distantly breathing the calm forest air,
restoring ourselves to joy
as the expectant couple
touched up their nest...

And then, as if reward for my many hand-sewn masks,
I received by the beleagured post
a box from my lancer
of edible, readable, and playable treats!

At this juncture I submit:
my day was as good as our vultures';
settling into covers
I thanked the distant lover
I haven't seen for months.

Apr 24
Dark Covers

Day as damp as our spirits
from overdosing on TV and, for me,
New Yorkers,
full of the good (Dr. Fauci) the bad (McConnell)
the ugly (right-wing funded plague protesters).
The magazine is dark. Black dominates the
covers,
as if wreaths were placed on all the doors
of all the apartments
for all the suffering.
Lamb's blood or no,
they weren't saved.
I'd gladly get out of the way for the young,
if that were the answer...
When so many starve
will I wish I had fed more?
Will it ever be enough?
Will I ever be worthy
to cling to this lifeboat?
Who will kick me off?
Would they feast on my flesh?
I'm not of the chosen,
clearly. I'm like some fat Donalds:
too stingy to die.

Apr 25

A Very Scary Doc Indeed

Pileated woodpecker wakes me from
the emerald forest dream,
drilling violently
as tree-cutters
that raze my forest home,
leaving me stranded on the last dead tree,
my baby-ape self the final image
in "Planet of the Humans,"
a film that reminds me
I'm not the only misanthrope.
Those baby orangutans
dying in the mud,
that stark lone tree
of Camus
who said "death embraced is liberation,"
and yes, *is* liberation
for the survivors who find a world
more manageable than the one before.

The scythe must be wide and swift!
I want to live to see the difference it makes.
I want to wake up in 2070 and smell the fresh air
free of Death of my generation.
The young generation,
(the one I live now through my children),
must hear the woodpecker
when I'm gone,
having happily ceded my time
in the emerald forest of our dreams.

Apr 26
A Whole Planet of 'Em

So I numb my brain
with some dumb TV.
What else is new? It's all
we'd see. From our baby days
to our dotage, we
join a world of apes dying on TV,
dying apes in the glare of stark arc lights,
watching dying apes all day and through the
night,
a chorus of apes sings "Ring-around-the-rosy" —
shakes to the sting 'til they fall.

Toll the churchbells:
"Wrong! Wrong! Wrong!"

Apr 27
Another Tuesday? Are We Sure?

Back on my bike, then walking with a friend,
even my absent lancer checks in!
A new-normal day of puzzles and news,
a bunch of Zoom meetings
an afternoon snooze,
a chat with old bud from a Midwest Red State
to get her perspective on the current debate:
should Biden choose Warren, or somebody
black?
Whoever she'll be, she had better not lack

the leadership skills we've been craving for
years.
Meanwhile, Phil Murphy and Cuomo get cheers.
Our dictator fumes as all dictators do.
May this late April Tuesday prove pleasant for
you!

Apr 28
Neanderthal Blues

Culture poured like wheat
into the threshing bin;
all day mad thoughts, as if in school lockdown,
the the shooter at large with its AR-15...

Anyone can write a book, a song, a play.
Neanderthals made paintings 65 thousand years
before
we noticed they were artists and our genes
were some of theirs. The human race,
the very culture, soup stock, dough
from which we've risen to see our end,
is sadly letting go of life, more so
today than when
our distant cousins sought refuge from
a plague of *sapiens*.

A White Whale Glimpsed

The night is stormy, windy wild.
I play with Melville's Gothic mind,
and though another genius child,
to call him "our Dante"'s much too kind.
As one neurotic to another,
I see a man oppressed by mother.
Yearning for love he found at sea
with sailors, how he longed to be
the bride of Billy Budd! As I
would have my Dante days and try
to work through all those doubts and pain
of aliens who toil in vain
to sail Shakespearean oceans while
attached to farmsteads and a pile
of papers one would gladly burn —
so glad I never had to earn
my keep by writing. How not to fail
at that — like hunting some white whale!
It seems the artists I love best
are more neurotic than the rest,
for wrestling with our demons makes
us feel productive and it takes
our minds off failed relations with
those we might love, so we might live
in balanced joy, as Willy did,
with mastery of tragedy
as much as that of comedy.
A smiley-frowny mask was he,
envy of his progeny.
For none shall beat the bard at this.

The time for poetry was his.
Our times are brutal and, so far,
degenerate; we simply are
reverting to pre-modern times,
reliving, as old Vico rhymes,
the new medieval darker days
where life is wasted as the sage.
Ol' Melville tried to make us see
our strife born of Confederacy.
We, too, see how the white whale thrives;
our plague has shown us that who dies
is predicated more on skin
and poverty — the poor can't win,
will die out first and we will learn
that though we might decide to burn
entire libraries of yore,
we'll be heading toward a time before
the internet and all its cant.
We'll find ourselves brought low by scant
amounts of electricity
(which Melville learned from Ms. Shelley
was much an animating force).
I trust him as a better source
of wisdom than a guy like Trump,
who represents this dire slump.
But from all ashes do arise
new miseries in new disguise.

Apr 30

The Cruelest Month Goes Out Like A Lion

The wind blows out this April's flame;
all up and down these streets untame.
Trashcans roll like tumbleweeds...
I give my body what it needs:
fresh air and movement in the world,
my mind at ease while branches hurled
upon the lawns as if to say:
"You've no control! Your feet are clay.
You've been brought low.
You feel the deer's
vigilance born of its fears?"
The Gothic mistral rules our town.
The lancer plans to send me ground
coffee as he's ascertained
I no longer grind the beans... I feign
the verse form of old Melville, who
was late romantic, just as you,
my lancer, are aspiring to
a goodness that transcends this flu,
or virus, as we call it now.
I'll make my scribblings anyhow
and in the morning, fueled on joe,
I safely through May's world will go.

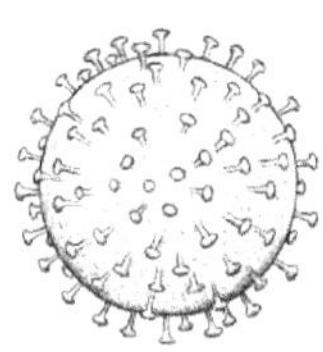

May 1
Bringing On the Leaves

Workers of the world rejoice in sunshowers!
Biking through this opulent suburban garden,
gathering bouquets of stolen flowers,
lilacs and wisteria perfume my rooms—all two
of them!

I shake off horrors of the damnedly poor,
realize there is little I can share.
My meager supports will not net me more;
with no inheritance, I must endure.
My kids should not bring babies where
they're bound to see more misery than I
through mere frustration with the wind and sky.
Today the sunshowered scintillating leaves
made for some psychedelic scenes abroad.
My bike and I got wet as children's sleeves
in strollers; grandmas, parents, teens and dogs
united in a rainbowless midday,
delightful moment caught out in the wild.
It's okay to take assault this way.
All will keep as mobile as we must;
some may melt while others merely rust.

May 2
College Re-Zoom-ion

The day of trippy greens,
when all the forest leaves are new,
reminded me of mushroomed scenes
when we collegiates barely knew
that we'd look old in 40 years
(and now it's nearing 45).
We met—a bunch of us—on Zoom
and though all very much alive
(most sitting in a living room
or in an ample backyard space)
we told each other it was hard
to live now as we're losing grace.
That is, the acid's wearing off
and now we fear that coming down.
Though none were heard to sneeze or cough,
I sensed a grimace, half a frown;
some Zoomers weren't enjoying this,
though I was not among that crowd.
For me the spring has been pure bliss—
more silent, yes, and much less proud.

May 3
Fun With Marx Bros

Today the commies came to chat,
first in France, then Trenton and
greater Jersey, as I sat and walked and talked
and sometimes ran into a bit of argument
about the future workers' plight:

that maybe we are on the verge
of something to restore the might
of proles who've lost so much and thus
would the ranks of owners purge...

They run and hide most cowardly;
those maskless rich themselves protect.
I wonder if they'll leave us stores
and farms and mills and factories
to commandeer and resurrect
and maybe find new purpose for.

I argue with my fellows that
would form the nascent movement's core.
We *could* rise now and lever just
enough weight on the system for
profit margins to go bust
(if unions *do* come back in style).
We could agree that now we're at
a place where workers might unite,
though organizing takes awhile...
and all my lefty friends are right!

May 4
Planning For Up-coming Work In CO

I bike and walk with different friends.
The lancer still has not come through
with invitation to commune
across a fire pit, as we do.
His silence suddenly offends.
I now make plans to fly away.

By June he'll have to let me go.
As I go off to work it ends—
affections that we fail to show.

May 5
Preparation

You know that feeling when you rise
from watching some escapist pap
and suddenly re-realize,
that while your brain was on its nap,
the virus out there killed and killed?
The moon grows fat as tallies rise
of neighbors gone too soon. We sing
new songs of heartbreak and demise.
We die alone... Death's glass is filled.
We watch our doctors for each sign:
a smile or wink not through a mask,
a loved one not confined to screen;
alas, we meet the great divine
alone, though ain't it always thus?
No matter what the cause each year,
we die and seldom make a fuss,
for at the end we lose our fear
and leap out of our damaged shell
as if embarrassed by its weight,
make a right turn out from hell
and speed direct through Peter's gate.

May 6
The Science of Garbage Disposal

Watching shows on wars and pedophile priests,
listening to lectures on how corporate capitalists
manipulate our evangelicals...

Considering how sick my country is,
Covid's just a green patina on
the body politic now terminal, and this
may be the best news yet: Don soon be gone!

The world panics in pandemic, this is true,
worse where they suffer lies, as here we do;
Wuhan cowards tried in vain to cover up,
the escaping virus never bound to stop.

We now have China's medical response
and all advancing real research at once.
Around the world, united as we are,
in fronts we'd never known without a war,
no priests will dictate healthy morals to
the minions who have every need to know
more *science* every day, and so,
with hope eternal sprung I bravely go...

May 7
Covid Be Damned!

At last I saw my lancer
as I'd imagined him:
grown-out hair ringing

his Roman forehead
like graying laurels,
sitting across the fire pit,
while the full moon
darted in and out of clouds
along with our dialog...

and it had been a sunny day
of walks and more exploring
well-trodden paths and empty streets
of suburban New Jersey
where we both began.
Covid central:
where one who's careful
can still make love —
well-worth the risk
when one *is* in love.

May 8
In Praise of Tech and Art

Watching a live performance of
Dancing in Lughnasa on Zoom:
the young actors costumed in their squares
emote into their devices
about the sonorous wonders
of the Marconi set of 1936,
technology that let Ireland dance
through the lead-up to WWII.

All we do now is improv:
shopping in masks while

inventively gripping our carts
with disinfectant wipes,
sanitizing our groceries before putting them
away.
We talk as much as possible by phone,
while listening to public radio discussions
about how to combat loneliness,
as if our updated Marconis
were our oldest and best friends.

May 9
New Fears in the Air

Cold — unseasonably so,
yet sun and windburn sweep
the unwelcome virus from our streets.
I walk with my masked friend from the
frontlines.
Tending to nursing home inmates, she
is braver than I,
who fear flying now,
not in the Jongian sense,
but for the air, imprisoned air,
maddened air, befouled air
exuded by my fellow passengers...
a sick, unseasonable wind.

Oh, the bus is smaller every year
and speeds faster, faster
with an expanding universe
all racing toward nothingness,
particles leaving each other,

pixels, points,
poof —
into the cavernous
gale.

May 10
On Mom

Sun and bloom:
so glad for mothers here
and those long in tomb
who met their rest
before our country failed this test
of democratic hopes and dreams
our mothers fought to guard.
It seems
the new world's dawning every day;
I wish the old would fade away
and take along the very old.
Let youth shine on
as mothers fold.

May 11
Estrangement Hurts More Now

A friend is hurting — says she must remain
estranged from only daughter. She complains
her daughter has not talked with her for years;
the silent treatment brings my friend to tears...
Is now not time to wonder if we are
restored in all relations, or yet far

from reaching out to tell the ones we love
the steadfast Power watches from above
and sees how hard we've tried to make amends?
The showdown of some wills will find no end
until the virus clears us and we're done;
the course of this harsh lottery's not run.
If making peace on our side were enough,
we could let go—yet letting go is tough
when such a knot of feelings, unresolved,
threaten to impede the course of love.
Perhaps the peace comes only with the loss...
I tell my friend I'm sure there is a Boss
who guides her daughter as she's guided to
have made enough amends when they were due
and now she must content herself with peace
that comes when will-collisions simply cease.
One day her daughter—should they both
survive—
will find her mom and fast their love revive.

May 12

Dear Doctor Please Help Us We're Damaged

Dr. Fauci tells the Senate we're
not out of woods yet—
oh, he's very clear
the virus bounces back
as folks return
to places we have let
them free to run
and watch as more fall down;
the virus won

the first round.
Now we take a little stretch
then start another inning
where we fetch our wallets
not our masks, commence to spend —
okay, that's fine, but who's prepared to fend
off crazies who would spread the germ about?
Methinks, the commerce we can do without.
As Fauci says, "use caution, take it slow" —
while lemmings to the cliff we gladly go...

May 13
Wishing for a Wormhole Out

Most TV shows look violent, not much fun:
psychokillers, crimes solved and some un-.
I watch a doc about astronomy.
It tells of the late discoveries
from fourteen years ago, by now-old men.
And so I research all developments since then.
The universe, it seems, is still quite flat
and dark energy — or is it dark matter? — is most
of that,
accelerating to infinity
with potential for regeneration locally
through those black holes, now observed,
while the human population, upcurved,
pursues its devolution toward the lout,
yet wishes for a wormhole out,
a "regeneration" if you please,
(please gods), just long enough past me
for my kids to grow old and decay.

Today they both seem better than okay.
Though dystopian visions haunt my son,
the daughter has more hope and thus more fun.
Her dark matter, (or dark energy?)
expands her far as she can see.
I watch the documentary that is them
with fascination, trepidation, laughs and tears,
and nowadays, especially, work to stem
the tidal pull of any mother's fears.

May 14
May is for Youthful Memories

A birthday of a boy I once so loved,
I barely slept the nights I'd been with him.
If only for a roll upon the grass...
I even climbed his fire escape that time,
to find him occupied with someone else.
Oh, he is gone to seed as all of us;
the "Olds" they call our class of hippie teens.
We went to college when it wasn't quite
as brutally elitist. If we'd known
we'd come to this joint where we waste today,
we'd be above our years, for no one young
can grasp the meaning of such memory
as would revive the very taste of time...
So languidly we'd sail home with the wind,
planing over waves, more light than foam...

____

May 15

The Virtues of Inactivity

I must confess my happiness:
this virus vindicates my sloth.
So lazy as the days grow warm,
a new routine that lets me lull
in bed and start the day with friends
appearing on my screen as I
lie naked, masked, from them by tape
across my laptop's camera eye,
then breakfast, coffee, news and calls
to other loved ones far and near,
then walks or bike rides in the wild
where Nature shows me her good cheer
for all the clearing, quiet skies,
the freshets chirping like the birds.
I come back to my cozy nook,
make meals, take naps, read books
and then, go searching for a final treat:
a movie or a special doc.
Last night I found the perfect show!
A twenty-four part lecture on,
tada: Black Death, and recent, too;
has all the latest scholarship!
It seems *that* plague was multiple,
as ours may prove, that is, not one
attacking horde of microbes, but
a coalition — armies of
bacterial *and* viral beasts,
ravaging port cities first,
then catching all the countryfolk,
just as here we're going through

the phase where Trump's towns fall as well,
all dominoes contiguous...

I finished Whitehead, who reminds
that God and lifeforce dance us back
from every sleep—we'll wake from this
old nightmare to rebuild anew;
and maybe *these* medieval days
will bear solutions yet unthought,
as then. I must work my way
through episodes beyond the sixth
to learn from experts how that plague
gave fourteenth century folk a fix
and Zoomed us to the modern age
so we could reach Aquarius.
The Endtimes are about to fade...
I'm happy—most delirious!

May 16
Zooming Around

Yet more reunions via Zoom:
around the world we're saying "Hi"
to friends and lovers once with whom
we'd shared a laugh, perhaps a cry,
while outside now the flowers bloom.
Irises I found and I
stole some—they bedeck my room—
while cycling. I found reasons why
I've taken up the poet's loom:
dotting meadow paths nearby
are poems where I did carom

by on my bike, though I did try
to capture some in camera's zoom
to read another time, rely
on wisdom as a fine heirloom.
And so, dear friends, we say good-bye,
as if to turn and face the tomb.
I've loved each verbal butterfly,
since creeping from my jeweled womb.

May 17
Boning Up on History

My lovely lecturer, Medievalist,
assures me plagues can bring about unrest
as well as innovations and reforms.
(I hope our plague conforms to ancient norms.)
Meanwhile, my ex- has almost bought a house,
while real estate and interest rates are low,
our daughter to be kept — a country mouse —
in sane Vermont, and while there go
toward graduate degree and better life
of earning and avoid the normal strife
of living job to job. Security
is nothing like we thought it once to be:
a grand illusion shared by nearly all.
In 1348 the sudden fall
of institutions stabilizing lives
begets a new regime in which one thrives
by simply skirting death, that nimble scythe
that misses some wheat strands while taking
tithe
from nobles, clergy, merchant and the least,

who far outnumber them and live to feast,
at last, in manor homes and abbeys void
of masters with whom canny fate has toyed.

May 18
Sad to Leave the Mid-Fourteenth for the Early
Twenty-first

Alas, I've come to the end of the Black Death —
that is, my 24 part lecture series that
reminded me we've seen all this before
and should anticipate more deadly waves...
Corona viruses are only one
class of lethal bug that shall attack,
and though today the vaccine seemed in sight
and stocks roared up in hopes, I hold no breath.
Such plagues are omnipresent, prevalent,
as somewhere in the world an outbreak hits.
We may not have the smarts to race ahead
when once again our numbers are reduced.
We could use a halving of our bulk
to usher in the new phase that once came
on heels of Rome's plague of Justinian
that welcomed in the stable reign of church,
which gave way in mid-fourteenth century.
Another 500 plus years and
we see a decimation once again,
resulting in the global world of now,
as if our wars were not enough to reap
the soul-fields when it's harvest time again.
It seems there is maintained in those who live,
variety, to reset life, along with some

continuity of types. Despite the cut, the same
general strata will remain.
I hope the working class moves up a notch
and maybe some advances in the arts,
some science and technology breakthroughs,
some protocols to better face each wave,
a lessening of viral strengths and some
new drugs to ward off killing off the young.
It's fitting that the old should slough away,
but *please* let *my* kids live past me in years.
And as old Petrarch wrote around the time
his twenty-something son had died of plague:
"To face death in fear is base weakness."
Let's hope some courage in our kind is left
and from the ashes raise a stronger crop,
acquainted with the horrors and more sure
that life should thence be lived with greater
heart.

May 19
I Know Good Poems When I See 'Em

My daughter sends me poetry sublime;
(she knows naught of this shoddy shallow
rhyme).
She thinks I'm delving deep into our plague,
not pissing 'round in circles sounding vague...
It's just that these times lack in gravity
because of Donald Trump's depravity.
How can we take a heartfelt turn at pen
when such inane reactions rise again
with Don each morning, as he tweets anew

his lamentations that this minor "flu"
is messing up his dictator's sick dreams,
while on each trauma floor a doctor screams
for everything that's lacking now to save
the lives a-tumbling toward each new mass
grave?
Today, as in Medieval times, I know,
when persons unaffected came to show
a callousness as yet unknown by those
who thought they knew them — now, do you
suppose
we, in this hour, are better for our wealth
and some advances in our state of health?
I see no end in sight as down we go.
And if this isn't poetry I sow,
it's good as juxtaposing on TV
Covid news with ads for colonoscopy
kits to take home for convenience.
The crazy lives we've led here make no sense
when new examined in blue viral light
that glows throughout each weary day and
night,
as if a comet *had* come to announce
that Nature had at last produced an ounce
of cure for Her affliction, meaning us —
to cram us Bozos in some speeding bus
and drive it neatly off the nearest cliff.
(No wonder lemmings are a common gif.)
We're laughing as we tumble like Trump's dice
through dead casinos never very nice,
failed and bankrupt as his dumb ideas.
Our nation folds in pestilent arrears,
owing more than it can ever pay

to workers, dying each pharma-ad-filled day—
as if the last thing one shall hear is not
a priest's confession, but a slick robot
insisting we go out right now and buy
our way back to heroic times that I,
for one, have never felt within this land,
inspiring as a patriotic band
playing rousing marching songs in war;
and this, at last, is what we're fighting for:
a chance to live—no more—and yet that lump
inside the White House takes daily dumps
on Twitter to lament a shifting base,
who'll leave him when they, too, have had to
face
that wailing mother/father/child or friend
who's lost a dear one and can not defend
the guy who told them this was but a hoax.
And so, my daughter, all my petty jokes
in doggerel reflect these TV times.
Should children's books retell this tale in rhymes
like "Ring Around the Rosy" and the one
about a sad pied piper who was done
with being jerked by fraudsters in that town
and so he piped the people's children down
into a cave, (which strikes me as a tomb,
for never did they come out from the gloom
to light the lives of elders of their day,
but rather stole their hope and joy away)?
All futures come with changes most profound
and poems tend to lay some thoughtful ground
for New Times as they dawn—I'll celebrate
the end of this regime and all its hate,
but not until it's over can I write

a thing of beauty, for in truth I might
misportray the tenor of these days,
as there is nothing to uplift or praise.

As I, too, gaze into that darkest cave,
I long for some poetics that could save
the good that was a part of this land too,
but that, my daughter, will be up to you.

May 20
But a Tease

My lancer came and went — all much too quick.
Complained he wasn't well,
but wasn't sick.
These days it's hard to find a friend to hold
on through the night, when nights have turned
quite cold
and floods have broken dams, (though not here
yet),
and everyone we love may someday get
this plague, though I will want to be the last.
I'm willing to be chronicler and ask
the heavens to forgive my foolish writ
all tied in knots like kerchiefs or a bit
of cloth to cover nose and mouth complete,
so kissing is a rather awkward feat.
If only we could cleave to those we love
and blow through plague like clouds that pass
above;
but no, our dams break as our hearts today
and as he did tonight, love slips away.

May 21
Maskless As Clueless

Well, despite much speculation from the press,
the Trumpster did what anyone could guess:
toured a Ford plant out in Michigan
without a mask, rejecting once again
appeals from workers to respect their health.
(Little Don cares only for himself.)
We're never going to get past this clown
until the virus takes his people down.
If he's too evil to give up the ghost,
then put him in our hell and watch him roast!
(He'd taste a lot like bacon, that's for sure.)
It's clear he's set us up for even more
dying citizens whose only crime
was going off to work to make a dime
preserving life, as we once valued life,
unlike the autocrat exempt from strife.
By virtue of a narcissistic shield,
the Maskless Wonder dominates the field,
while in his basement quietly below,
the brew is rising for one "Sleepy Joe."

May 22
New War Declared

We call it "war" because of strain
of living day to day with stress.
We wince at every ache and pain.
Our stomachs churn; our head's a mess.
There's tension through each waking hour

as news seeps in. No matter how
we try to coat dark thoughts with flour,
we gorge and vomit anyhow.
I see how even I am bent
from carrying this novel weight
without a partner or a gent
to back me up, and yet my fate
is not to whine for what is gone.
I've had it all, and more, you see.
My lancer may just be the last
and now I fear that even he
is twisted by this coiling force
and damaged by abiding fears.
I rue another fake divorce,
(we've been a thing for nigh five years).
I must give way to war and loss
and every day pass o'er my bridge,
from which my round white pebbles toss,
and pray we all retake the ridge
before we're shot down in the mud...
this is a war of flesh — not blood.

May 23
Memorializing Makes Sense

For once, a gray Memorial Day
suitable for grief. Too damp;
we want to picnic and cannot
do more than feel this tragedy.
But Yankees don't do tragedy.
There is no loss but net loss here.
There is no grief but passing sighs;

grief takes stages one through five.
We skip ahead to work today.
We are workaholics all.
Work, work, work so not to feel..
Now we'll see what work there is,
as jobs evaporate like rain,
the low-wage earners are destroyed.
New desperate ones will soon replace
the lowly, who must always die,
while gritty, canny ones go on,
the sloppy self-indulgent, no.
Irresponsibility does kill.
The privileged and the paranoid
are ours to fear as they must win.
Some lock us in, some fight us off;
we'll not break down their castle walls.
We grieve the loss of power to
feed our kids and build anew.
If this is it, then let's be done
with grief, and sing out everyone!

May 24
Resenting the Reckless

Walking today in a popular park,
the sky was bright but my mood turned dark.
The Great Unmasked breathed in my face,
this carelessness a vain disgrace!
So what if others get my germs?
So what if they can't come to terms
with our mortality? I feel
as if my neighbors can not deal

with life in this calamity.
Like Jews who grant the cruelty
of Nazis breaking windows as
"just the other guy's" — not those we love,
seems families can love a crowd
of their vast kin, so party proud
while never seeing *me* go past.
I swear, I hope to be the last
soul standing as they all fall down,
though this will be a ghostly town
and not much fun when one day soon
they heed the piper's cunning tune
and vanish, leaving me to cry...
I wish they'd seen me — cared that I
not catch from them the plague they ply,
while *I* mask to save the *other* guy.

May 25
Innocence Found

Here appeared a child's drawing
with trees colored "green,"
skies "robin's egg blue,"
clouds as only a child would make:
impossibly fluffy and white.

Beachgoers take virginal steps into
the still-cold sea.

Charcoal smell in evening light,
quiet save for ambulance.

When we memorialize this time:
not quite summer, fulsome spring,
it is with shame we find ourselves
no longer children, crayons clenched,
but armies set out to destroy
the innocence of all that's green,
and craft new winter here.

May 26
Dreaming of Dead

I see you coming toward me, my dead.
You are leading with your mouths,
the mouths through which our doughnut selves
take in the world then spit it out.
I sleep with my mouth open, my tongue dry.
I can well imagine the old-lady corpse I'm
rehearsing to be.
Oh, I'm not sad to be on this slow train,
more conscious every day,
how it flips the bowels
connected through this tunnel
to my mouth, so as I turn, my insides
become my outsides.

May 27
On Surviving On

The scientists assure us there will be
a new normal and reality
wherein we'll be adapting to this bug,

and soon, I trust, get rid of ruling thug
whose tolerance for facts and truth is nil —
he thinks he'll cure us with some worthless pill!
But I know, as some science guys tell me,
that's not the coming new reality,
wherein we learn to live with Covid and
the myriad expressions of its brand.
We may not have a cure for centuries,
especially if penitentiaries
persist, like nursing homes and schools,
to harbor viruses and fools
who won't refuse to work there, though the threat
of dying on the job is one sure bet.
I can't imagine there will be an end
to life with Covid, as I can defend
myself for years. I hope and trust today,
(though all my hope and trust may blow away),
if one I loved did sicken and succumb,
I'd quickly go insane or merely numb
and stumble like a zombie through this hell
that I have come to master rather well.

May 28
Healthcare Heroes Emerge for Us to Sing

"A cacophony of coughing" the young ER
doctor said.
The horrors of this war, acute,
ring in the ears, exploding shells
of lives snuffed out despite all work.
All work in vain, not what they sought,

while training years to learn their skill.
There's been at least one suicide, a young girl doc,
who'd had no way to end the torture in her head.
It seems the "heroes" we applaud
are merely human; it's too hard
to keep it up—all soldiers need
some R&R. I wish them all
some time to grieve and catch their breath.
This is a war where new recruits
are hard to train, though train we must
the next green troops... Goodbye med school.

May 29
O E.M. We Need You Now!

I end this day with *Howard's End.*
This movie always makes me think
that Forster'd be the perfect friend.
I'd raise a glass to him and clink
for humanists 'round every bend,
who knew that love is found in most
of all who find they can be kind...
To Edward I shall give this toast:
"For honoring the female mind!"

Women, if they once could rule,
would turn this sorry world around
and tame each narcissistic fool
that knows not where the heart is found.
That women have compassion for

the poor and suffering is known.
Some men have yearnings but for war
and claiming rights to gold and throne.
But now we're seeing who is gold:
the women caring for the sick.
They feed the poor, and some are bold
enough to play at politick.
It seems the nations doing best
have women captains at the helm,
while here, Testosterone's Wild West,
the rogue males tend to overwhelm
with cold brutality and vice.
I've said it more than once or twice:
we're learning lessons every day
through real hard knocks—the only way.

May 30
A Day in the Life Preparing for Death

The penultimate day of this fabulous month is
splashed with peonies and paint.
I worked on shutters with a brush and saw the
vultures' nesting place,
then met with folks in Ireland I'd never seen
until today.
The Zooming fills me full of hope that we might
find a better way.
Then on to walking with a friend in cooling
streets with other blooms,
then laughing with comedienne, whose
brilliance lit my living room.

Now off to bed, forget the plague, forget the
riots in the towns
where mobs are burning headquarters where
once police would hold them down.
And how exempt am I from this? I feel I'm
floating in the clouds...
The riots haven't made it here, perhaps our
streets are not that proud.
And yes, I listen to the news and follow all our
tragedies,
but in my little fairy world it feels like none
apply to me.
And yet I still prepare for death and bid my fond
ones much adieu.
I'd like to pass the acid test: go down blooming,
brave and true.

May 31
I Host the Real Memorial Day

Okay, we're back to normalcy;
we had a picnic in the park
with friends for weeks I'd dared not see:
a joy sublime, a social lark!
And yet a few things were off key,
like sanitizing hands and not
sharing plates, and masks would be
cumbersome, sometimes forgot.
We tried to keep our distances
and cover up when passing close,
though many were insistences
that naught was spewed from mouth or nose.

The food was excellent, well grilled,
the breeze kept germs from hanging 'round.
As hostess I was more than thrilled
that life has somehow come around
to what felt sane and wholesome, as
the month of May gives into June,
with ring-around-the-rosy as
the game we play 'neath waxing moon.

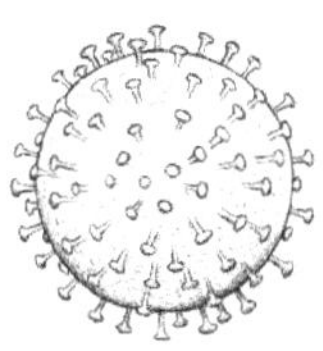

Jun 1

From the Garden of Earthly Delights

Now I must write my faithful rhyme
(though there is little new to say);
that Bosch was early for his time
depicting Hell as we today
see minions crowded o'er our land,
tall buildings in the distance rise,
the tortured reeling with the damned
as music blends with human cries.
Our cities flood with angry mobs;
at last it's coming to a head.
So many wail: "We've lost our jobs"
and "Another black man now lies dead
among us on the filthy street,
where we must meet to air our woes..."
I pray white racists meet defeat.
A corner turned?
Do you suppose?

Jun 2
Princeton Takes the Streets

Out on my bike this evening, I
found protesters marching by.
I joined them and wove through the town.
Police escorts were all around —
even K-9 — silly when
you realize Princeton, now and then,
turns out to show some sympathy
with movements in which we can see
a small resemblance to our burg,
a place where eggheads ponder these
expressions of the greater seas
and tides of race and their disease...

But one guy'd lost his sanity,
marched ranting at humanity,
alone reciting history
and "Black Lives Matter"
in dashiki!
Thank gods he'd joined us marchers late,
for now I hear him, still irate,
three hours later — through the park:
his skin is light, his soul is dark...
(Sings Ole Paul Robeson from the grave:
"That's one white ass we could not save.")

Okay, okay, we do our best;
and children's presence might attest
to future moments of unrest
attended here with less reserve...
(You don't need madness to have verve

and act in solidarity
with folks who seek equality.)

Jun 3
Intense Rainstorm at Island Beach State Park

Today off to the beach I stole
(and will not tell a single soul).
I went communing with my gods
and marvelously beat the odds
of walking back just as the sky
turned dark and raindrops fell, though I
was safe and sheltered in my car,
and though I didn't drive that far,
the storm swept up and threatened all
who'd braved the beach and found a stall
to summer plans in surf and sun...
I beat it back with everyone
who crossed the bridge in torrents now.
I made it home intact, and how
lucky to have found sea glass:
brown, white, green, blue to fill the glass
vase that holds my pieces safe.
No helicopters tried to strafe
us Jerseyans upon our beach,
though we were surely within reach
of guardsmen facing protesters
around the world, as crime festers:
the fascists beating on the poor.
And then Obama told the score
on nightly news — a Zoom-style meet
of blacktivists — I felt complete.

A day of Nature *and* great speech!
(And no one knows I'd hit the beach.)

Jun 4
Research on Racial Attitudes

Watched *Dear White People* just to see
what college kids are like today.
Is this how young black bourgeoisie
dresses, coifs and likes sexplay?
I saw no diff 'tween black and white,
(though writers made these kids sound smart),
elite's elite and might makes right.
What these kids mostly lacked was heart.
Contrasted with the gritty mobs
who've manned these streets, most lacking jobs,
protesting, teargas in their eyes,
it should not come as much surprise
that fancy colleges are not
effective places to work out
one's politics and learn the truth —
I rue the rich and coutured youth.

Jun 5
Sweet Contemplation of Separation

Wish my lancer would let me see him,
if only to say a sweet goodbye;
he'd played me "Girl from the North Country..."
He knows to make me moan and sigh,

but he is proud and needs to be
alone with all his solitudes.
I've stuck with him for years to see
if I'd break through his testy moods.
We live on edges, knives and spears;
we face the fascists through our fears,
and yet I fear I'll leave in tears
if he won't see me tomorrow.

Jun 6

The Last to See Me In the Low Country

If only I could share with you
the drive tonight toward setting sun
in Just June, the perfumed damp
infused with rolling meadows,
border woods,
farm fields between us.

And how a freight train holds me at the crossing
just a minute from your house;
you, too, can listen to the clack of cars along with
"Dear Prudence" through my windows.

And how when I arrive your peonies,
bent by rain,
call attention to your beds
and I, with peonies in hand,
a coal train from Newcastle,
enter your door.

If only you could come with me,
as I leave your warm kitchen at midnight
to encounter the full moon in your driveway —
gaze, hesitating — go back in? Steal another
hour?
(Though you'd yawned and we'd said our
goodbyes.)

You are the best anti-romantic
for my wild self-starring bio-pic:
the seductive, dark lead to my
Dorothy Parker big-hearted blond...

If only we'd synced our bodies with our minds,
but we were savoring the sweet goodbyes
because, though you try hard to act as blind,
you, too, are moved,
romantic in your guise:
the bold wood-chopping gardener
who sniffs his peonies and
lets them fall to Jersey's mud —

Damn the moon's chastising stare!
You've had the satisfaction when
you planted them precisely where
you'd be sure they'd bud again.

ROCKY MOUNTAIN NATIONAL PARK
SEASONAL EMPLOYMENT BEGINS

Jun 7
Arriving in Denver — Direct Flight

Flying with masks and sanitizing gel,
driving with phone GPS to Boulder hotel,
shopping in a store called Sooper,
meeting up with a long-lost friend: super-
duper!
Seeing snow-capped mountains, cottonwoods...
breathing Ponderosa pine,
stretching out with joy divine
and other new-bought wholesome goods.

Jun 8
Happy Birthday from 12,000 Feet!

Exhilarated as I was exhausted,
drove 24 miles up into the mountains,
found the store where I'll be employed
surrounded by glaciers,
moose and elk stops along the way,
good photo of two bucks grazing,
then back to meet some of the crew,
share pix,
check in with loved ones,
remember Dad would've been 96 today:
a man of the sea, he wouldn't relate.
*"El arroyo de la sierra, me complace mas que el
mar..."*

Jun 9
Getting Used to New Winds

As hard as we try
our workplace won't be
Covid-controlled nor, I fear, Covid-free.
I shudder to think I'll be first one to fall;
meanwhile I'll work here, keep eye on this ball.
Up in these Rockies the wind wails non-stop.
Not used to altitude, sense I could drop.
But the boss says she'll back me...
I hope she won't be
the last one to see me.
But hey — food here's free!

Jun 10
From My New Bigscreen Color TV

At last George Floyd has gone to blessed rest,
while his brother put the Congress to the test.
Will laws be changed before election day,
or will the great momentum blow away
along with souls who'll ride the viral wind
as we return to play with kith and kin?
I love my Rocky Mountain interlude:
the walks with wildlife, new friends, filling food,
but as we all go back to face the fall
without George Floyd, our don will take us all
beneath his outsize knee and lean down hard.
T'will be a tough tune for a happy bard.

Jun 11
Meditation at Mary's Lake

Thank you, Death, for coming when you did
to make life so much sweeter.
It was you we were missing all these years.
I'm tired of pretending,
of turning my back on you.
It's your job and privilege to make vivid
all the glories:
sun sparkles on the lake
lit by wind,
breath of the planet.

As I breathe You watch over my shoulder.
I have so many breaths to count to reach my
quota.
If You weren't watching now I couldn't know
or care about the wisdom of sun dazzles,
which would be lost to me...

If you didn't reap your harvests with vigor,
this lake would silt and stagnate.
Sun sparkles when the wind kisses the water.
I sparkle when You, Death, kiss me awake.

Jun 12
First Real Workday With the New Crew

Started work today — worked hard and long,
ate heavy supper, took brief walk, now hear the
song

of news reporters chorusing in minor key:
it seems the Covid outbreaks are what we
thought we'd see.
And now, though masked all day without a lull
and riding in a crowded bus then dining in a
room quite full,
I'm about to meet the public mask-to-mask
hoping in the power of plexiglass.
It all seems rather iffy and I'll have to pray
I get through months like this, Covid at bay.

Jun 13
My Days Off Will Now Be Wednesday and
Thursday — Fine With Me

My first day off, I walked out past the sign
that warned a mother elk defending calves
could trample me should I become a threat,
a black man who could bumble into cops
that might conclude I was most dangerous
and trample me in "self-defense" without a calf
in sight — can this be right?
My lancer says we must get over "rights,"
that right to liberty and happiness are null.
Does the mother elk have rights to kick
a tourist in her path she deems a threat?
I wonder at the protests, will they bear
outrageous outbreaks of this virus where
the notion that a fight for rights is worth
one's life — again — as always it must be?
For I am cowering by my new TV,
admiring protesters safe-distantly;

I like some space between myself and all
defensive creatures — be they great or small.

Jun 14
Co-worker Worth Talking To

Worked with a bright young thing today,
oped the teacher cage in me;
we talked of books and film and found,
though more than 40 years between,
we breached the gulf and shared our love
of looking through cosmology
to see as far as we can see...
And she will be the boss of me
when we start opening our store
to public traffic in the morn.
I hope I can my duties learn,
my young friend's trust to win and earn.
Glad she wants no children, for
the future holds adventures and
she's far too thoughtful not to know
the trials kids would face and so
she studies life and learns and grows
and thus becomes her own reward.
I hope all young ones live beyond
the reach of viral tentacles
(of course, there's fungi waiting, too,
as well as other germs still new).
We'll all go forth as best we can,
while stumbling o'er the ruins of man.

Jun 15

First Workday at 12,000 Feet

I gazed on alpine beauty feast...
then worked my butt off live-long day.
The Court gave workers' rights — at least
now LGBTQs can play
in capital and be defiled
just like all us cis work-schmoos
and all the live-long day I smiled
to get this morning's happy news.

Jun 16

Work: Love It or Leave It

We are a team. We dance the dance:
the dance of spit and cough and sneeze,
the masque of Death wherein the play
involves a bus on which we stay,
all faces bare, but mine, and Jim's.
I fear my colleagues, (hers and hims),
who gaily go about their day
as if this bug has danced away,
but no, it spreads like prairie fire
and who will get this flu most dire?
I hope not I, but I am not
the type this virus has forgot;
it's risk to me is greater than
to most our workforce, and the plan
to social distance, mask and glove
has *not* been danced — I live on love...

Jun 17
Texts from My Lancer Greet Meet Each Day
After Work

The guy back home insists I take a look
at all the big reveals in Bolton's book.
I argue that there's nothing we don't know
and that it's simply time to overthrow
that monster kleptocrat who'd rob us blind
if We-the-people gave him much more time.
His minions, still unmasked, are on the loose,
(and on the way to work I saw a moose).
Yet, methinks, the boyfriend's feeling good;
would share his optimism, if I could,
that Biden will gain *mucho* from John's screed.
(I'm working hard for dimes, myself, indeed!)

Jun 18
Weather Inconstant

Clouds swarmed at our mountaintop today
and snow fell as the bus drove us away.
In icy and slick patches cars passed by;
we stayed perversely quiet knowing why.
The world can bring on dangers fast and fierce
our usual bravado for to pierce.
And oh, the little crew, though stout most days,
did on this bus trip hunker down and pray.

Meanwhile, another rightwing pol rants on...
his loyalists now one by one have gone,
and even Facebook blocked his campaign ads

that used the Nazi symbol for those lads
and lasses who were once condemned to die
opposing Hitler then; now you and I
will represent the red triangle gang.
I hope Don's monsters go out with a bang!

Jun 19
Door Duty With Clicker-counter

Juneteenth — and up there in the store
I worked as people-counter at the door,
for Covid calls for limits as to space,
demands there'll be a mask on every face.
All day I waited, hoping once to see
a sight heart-warming as that mother elk
whose newborn struggled just to walk...

All day I clicked tourists lest one would be
a dark face coming in our mountain store.
Oh, we had white countenances galore,
a bunch of Asians, North and South,
distinguished by their eyes (since covered
mouth),
then finally, escaping midday snow,
in the company of white friends, (dontcha
know),
I'd happily admit one black-skinned man,
my secret Juneteenth celebrant who can,
unlike myself, appreciate this date,
on which the Texas slaves were told their state
had finally joined others to set free
the slaves whose torture shouldn't have to be

repeated like a dose of mountain snow...
By now, at last, this special date we'd know.

Jun 20
Panicked Symptoms

Could this be it? Could this be it?
Is this the dreaded coughing fit?
Got a headache that won't quit...
if Covid, I'm in deep, deep shit!
They've put some staff in quarantine.
Are they sick? What does it mean?
We go to work with fingers crossed;
it's hard to argue with the boss,
who thinks we can't enforce mask rule.
I think she should, that she's a fool
to jeopardize us all this way.
Forget the job! You keep the pay!
Am I just tired? A mere headcold?
How can we know if we're not told
results of tests we'll never get?
At least it's now a safer bet
that Trump won't last a second term
thanks to his evil, and this germ
that kept his latest rally seated.
Just like this bug, he'll be defeated!

Jun 21
Summer Solstice

The solstice came in sun and clouds;
the park was spared the season's crowds
as Covid shut down so much stuff.
A bighorn sheep up on a bluff
stared down on me and our work bus...
good for the park, not so for us.
The animals and plants can thrive
as humans fight to stay alive.
It's our turn to withstand the test.
Let Mother Nature do her best.

A HAIKU INTERLUDE:

Jun 22

Barr fires Berman.
Ten thousand cyclists clog streets.
So much to protest!

Jun 23

Funeral for Brooks,
shot in Wendy's parking lot.
Covid kills like cops.

Jun 24

Fauci warns: new surge.
Masks are not for everyone;
only the smart live.

Jun 25

Trump's "Kung Flu" sounds right
to his forty percent base
that holds us hostage.

Jun 26

SCOTUS must repeal
the ACA, just as we
succumb to Trump's will.

Jun 27

One-twenty-five-K
deaths are spiking, yet we don't
care to heed science.

Jun 28

Vlad pays Taliban
bounties for our soldiers' scalps;
Don shrugs allegiance.

Jun 29

"Ten million cases!"
cries the viral world today.
"Free caged kids at wall!"

Jun 30

Where states mandate masks,
Trumpsters mock as evil Dems,
good folk who wear them.

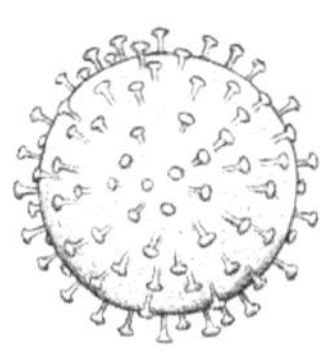

Jul 1

OSHA won't protect
healthcare workers dying now,
lacking PPE.

Jul 2

One-twenty-eight-K:
"It will sort of disappear,"
says Prez to echo.

Jul 3

Doctors plead: "Stay home,"
July 4th can barbeque
itself this summer!

Jul 4

The map grows redder:
virus spreads to all except
states that learned in spring.

Jul 5

Becky, Karen, Ken,
you know who you are and why
you scapegoat Black men...

Jul 6

U.S. Cases surge:
Trump reminds us "ninety-nine
percent are harmless."

Jul 7

Haiku section ends
with hopeful headline pipelined:
Standing Rock wins case!

Jul 8
Disney Plus

Watching "Hamilton" courtesy of Disney;
rich boyfriend says he'll reimburse me.
He'll watch it too, though he saw the stageplay.
I'm off work, having a great free day.
Note King George, he comes on like a Trump who
brags too loud about how he'll soon bump you
from your nascent democracy.

I hope the minions now will see
the king's a joke—he's got no clothes—
and Trump's pink ass we'll fast expose.

Jul 9
Cleanup Crews

Supreme Court rules: We're back to basic law
now
checking the exec—he's not above the law now.
Hope Cy Vance, can hurry to grand jury,
expose Trump's taxes, throw him into fury,
help us send the dictator to prison,
get past Trumpdom, restore the U.S. vision
of balanced powers—no runaway exec now,
keep justice system from odious train wreck
now.
Biden will have even more to clean up
than any Dem who has to follow screw ups
like Bush and Reagan, Repubs who cause
destruction.
Let's end Don on a note of cold conviction:
he should die in jail of case of Covid!
Let's have hope now, sing a song like Ovid
of times restored—of times of true progression.
Let's move on, end plague and its recession.
While we're at it, bring on reparations;
let justice cure all that call this jilted nation
home.

Jul 10
Stone Free

As much as yesterday's justice felt real good,
now it's clear again we've stood
all too briefly in the light,
as Trump commutes R. Stone tonight.
Another crony scoots away;
will justice yet be served one day?
If all of DT's wrecking ball
keeps swinging 'til the end of fall,
it's not so clear we'll ever blast
this monster, whose dank stain will last...

Jul 11
Home Remedy

All day my nose dripped on my mask...
it was a chore to pull each task
with fears of Covid haunting me.
'Twas fear that caused more misery;
but bath and vaporub and drugs
I substituted for sweet hugs.
Early night and plenty prayin':
"Covid be gone!" (I'm just sayin'...)

Jul 12
"Worst since the Great Depression"

The cure went well; I woke revived.
The day went fine, and lo — I thrived!
Though one more worker was dismissed.
(It seems the manager was pissed.)
I then watched *Perry Mason*, who
was groveling — a sad gumshoe
in 1931 Depression.
Workers take note; learn this lesson:
when times are hard and crime is high
we kiss our pride and hopes goodbye,
toil for "The Man" who cares
not one whit, and no one dares
give up his place at feeding trough.
Like 1931 — it's rough!

Jul 13
Mother Earth's Space Detectors

The tundra sports a Very Small Array
of bold sunflowers angled to the sun
as if alert to signals from deep space,
so close are they to regions far beyond...

Meanwhile, below, the sheeple struggle on,
their herd diminished by a virus not
from outerspace, but from dear bats,
who work for Gaia to control
her fruited plains, and will not rest

until our Mother's birthing pains
of some new nuisance calls her to
triage us pests with fatal flu.

Jul 14
Vive la Revolution!

Allons enfants de la patria...
you know the revolution's here.
Don't let the Don destroy your healthcare
and take away your rental home.
I think we workers might yet rise up.
We could defeat them if we dared.
We're never going to get wise, though,
because we're permanently scared.
The Big Boss is due to visit
our mountain Covid-ridden store,
but I won't be there when he comes in;
I'm off tomorrow and one day more.
We work so hard we're nodding out on
the bus ride down the mountainside.
I'm sure the Big Boss will be pleased,
not notice how our store's diseased.
As workers we can take some pride
in making him his handsome profits
as we risk our lives inside.

Jul 15
A Little Bearish

Today I climbed a little hill
like Maurice Sendak's Little Bear,
but I did not try to fly, even to the moon.
I'm not ambitious or a risk-taker;
hiking far into the park alone is not me.
Instead, I capture a hummingbird
sipping on a thistle,
gather sage to make smudgers
for my girlfriends as gifts,
from the long-gone prairie,
in the time of Covid
when a little magical cleansing
may be in order.

Jul 16
Magi

My friend came to visit me today;
he lives in Boulder, not far away.
We spoke of death with some humility.
We agreed we'll never know how we
will handle dying when it's done,
but now we thrive and so had fun.
We've lost our parents, some dear friends.
We both believe our fate depends
on random things we can't control.

A far friend sees me in a role
most tragic — mission: suicide.

Her feelings she refused to hide;
she'd miss me when I'm gone and I
assured her I don't want to die.
She thinks the risk I take's too great.
I say I've owned my risk and fate.

My friend from Boulder tells me he
will come again —I hope that we
can share more of my off-days here.
It sure was nice to bend his ear...

And then my lancer got in gear
insisting I indulge in some
TV show he loves and come
along in mind and spirit, so,
on one last night's adventure go,
because I love him and obey,
(it's one more silly game we play).

Thus ends 48 free hours.
Now back to work! Let's hit the showers!

Jul 17
A Goad from Joad

"They can't wipe us out;
they can't lick us; we'll go on forever
'cause we're the people..."
TCM showed *Grapes of Wrath*,
Ford's classic with Fonda as Steinbeck's hero.
Well, I'm a Commie now
and when I get back to Trenton

I'll resume organizin'
the service-class people.
This job helps to teach me,
though it seems like I'm slumming.
My fate's not to deep dive,
but skate, catching glimpses.
My spirit flies under or over or by,
and now — in a text — my lancer's reply:
"I will!"
a secret, soul-bolstering thrill!

Jul 18
Antlered Invaders

This day began when elk invaded
parking lot and lodging grounds.
We stood and clicked at them then waded
through their numbers to sit down
upon our bus, in which we travel,
up, up, up into the skies,
which on return are gray and threatening.
Lightning in the distance strikes
and wind, as if a gale, comes gusting,
yet, back at the lodge the elk,
still the grassy grounds are mowing...
Then, at last, the storm is quelled.
A rainbow spreads above the mountains;
once again we cameras click.
Was it something rare, auspicious?
Or just this day the elk herd picked?

Jul 19
The Beat Goes Wrong

Don sends stormtroopers to Portland
to *disappear* some guys.
Meanwhile, we mourn John Lewis,
and wouldn't it be wise
to stand up for some freedom
before the flag goes down?
I guess you'd have to be 'em —
Trump's over-eager clowns.

Jul 20
Stranding

The bus departed after work today,
leaving me alone at mountain store.
Thankfully, a landline worked to say
I needed a ride down, and then, what's more,
the day was just about as perfect
as Rockies' sunny summer days could be.
I wasn't sorry to be left to linger...
and supper, down below, was held for me!

Jul 21
Cashiered

A perfect day as jockey of my till:
two hundred some transactions
I'd fulfill;
then, miracle of miracles I found

my balance was a perfect whole. Then 'round
sunset, as the day was letting go,
I let myself feel tired and lay down.
The Trumpster — though he never will be fired —
is going, like the sun now,
down, down, down.

Jul 22
Catching Up With Loved Ones on My Day Off

As the nation broils and boils in wrath,
I had a day of happy news.
None yet hath writ my epitaph
and many whom I love now choose
healthy, joyous things to do:
buy a house,
birth a child,
learn to fly,
explore the wild...
(that last was me —
I gathered flowers
to press in hopes of making cards
to write my news and pass the hours,
thus share the merry life of bards).

Jul 23
Mountain Thunder Redunder

Thunder rolled and rain hit hard,
the first real rain this month.
The President is on the run.

He's losing everywhere.
The flowers needed watering.
The people need relief.
I spoke to loved ones far and near,
felt not a drop of grief.

Jul 24

Firing or Resignation?

Some say we've reached the end of the Road to
Tyranny.
Trump's dress rehearsal in Portland's streets
portends his election day response:
his jackboots must intimidate,
disrupt, and foil democracy.
I seek distraction in my work;
the daily grind now comforts me,
but here, in microcosm we
have lost another from our crew,
a young supervisor who
never seemed to find her feet.
And now we breathe a little sigh
as herstory tolls far and near.
I hope I land in State of Grace
and have no dictator to fear.

Jul 25
High Up With Santa

Some say it's Christmas in July;
shoppers act as much:
buy Xmas baubles, balls and such,
while down below the chaos spreads,
the cries are carried through thin air.
A coworker is carried down
to hospital—the altitude
gets to her—it's quite a perch.
I'm peering out into the gray;
rainclouds dominate the day
and shed tall tears upon the low,
the lowly and those who won't grow
old in Covid Days.

Jul 26
No Texts for Days

Still ghosted by the lancer—
must have scared him off again...
Meanwhile, we'd a break in rain.
Twenty-somethings rose 'fore dawn
to climb the highest Rocky peak,
and here I work and face the hoards
of shoppers, who keep rolling in
like clouds of viral load and leave
a trail of credit card receipts.
I cheer the end of Capital
and yet I fear it in defeat.
There seems no end to Fascist Days,

though summer's fading like our love.
I wish and wish for better ways
'prisoned at my till above.

Jul 27
Tundra Ladies Dance for Me

Today, on break, I watched the wind
tousle tundra flowers white
and yellow, far as I could see
beneath a cloud of mountain height,
as all looked up and out and down
and not at man so small, so brief.

Our President's a Devil found
in fiery depths that roil beneath.

Jul 28
I'll Take Any Text

At last! My lancer deigns to text
and nothing personal at that.
I go to sleep in new context
of hope — he hasn't left me at
that "altar" where he'd said "I will"
and run for hills as high as mine.
I must admit I get a thrill
no matter what he says — it's fine;
he knows I have the next days off
and I have waited eight whole days
to wonder if he's caught a cough

or gotten sick in other ways,
or found a friend to comfort him —
(I wouldn't blame him if he had) —
yet leaving me out on a limb
in times like these is simply bad.
I'd love to ask him about Barr,
who lied and lied in House today
and scary shit they've done thus far
to keep democracy at bay,
but he is insecure and now
I fear I left him more confused;
I wonder if he's found out how
he'd come out here, not be refused...
I wish I could assure him that
my love for him is mountain high
and steadfast as the hunting cat
who'd rather play than watch prey die.

Jul 29
Empty Stands

Covid baseball's weird and slow-motion:
13 innings with just four runs,
creepy soundtrack of noisy crowds
echoing empty stadium...
Worked on presents, cards and such,
walked to town and back in heat,
glad to talk to far-off friends,
get text from lancer yet again —
a day of R&R indeed!
A lot of solo time I need.

Jul 30
I Stand Accused

Today the boss accuses me
of being anti-social — well!
She is, herself, a Nature Girl,
avoids the crowds and I could tell
it was a chiding I could take
and took it for another day
of creative room-bound play.
Walk to beleaguered P.O. to
mail out my gifts to those I miss;
I hope he likes the bit I wrote,
but pleasing other's not a note
I need to hit all day and night.
Both the boss and I are right.

Jul 31
My Favorite Marmot

Charlie the Marmot's a family man;
3 marmot pups now cavort by our store!
Tonight the boss chastised the kids
for careless acts and disrespectful talk.
I'm now relieved to know that's why
the mandatory supper meeting called.
The chief was not
so angry that she didn't serve
us "thank you" cake and chocolate bars.
A rainbow met us as we left
the crowded dining hall —
that Covid hub — gods save us all!

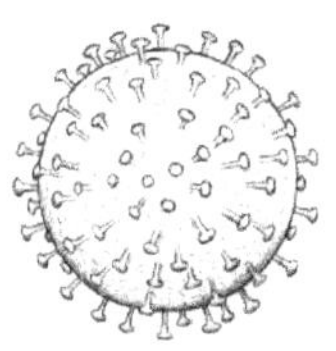

Aug 1
Life of Marmots

In boom and howl
of last night's storm,
I thought of marmots safe and warm
in leaf-lined burrow at the peak
and though her kittens can but squeak,
the mother nursed them in the sun,
their legs akimbo — oh, what fun
to watch these babies while they lunched,
the mother proud and barely hunched
above her squirming, feisty brood...
It seems she thinks we're something good
protecting her and witnessing
maternal triumph — not a thing
to go unwitnessed, so we shot
a video of them and got
back to work to end the day
with news the Trumpster's bound to play
more dirty tricks before he's through.
I'd stick with marmots — wouldn't you?

Aug 2
Still Obsessed With Outsized Squirrels

Now I dream of rodent kits
that turn to human children and
I notice where there once were 3
there seem to be but 2 at lunch...
Ferocious mountain thunder storms
and rainbows come and go with ease.
I wonder if a hawk swooped down
and snatched the third, or if the 3
trade places, playing in and out
of burrows — oh, I stress as if
I were a marmot mother in
a Rocky Mount apocalypse.

Aug 3
If You Knew How Cute They Are...

Again, just 2 kits make my day...
All moms concern themselves with school:
will we, won't we send to play
our darlings? And there's not one rule;
all must decide and most will be
as lost as marmots on this cliff.
If I had kits I'd never cease
to watch them close — and worried stiff —
allow them out to peek about,
yet keep them near the burrow where
I can control them, banish doubt
about their health. I'd never dare
allow them too much scope right now.

No human mother knows just how
to keep her kids safe while at school;
the marmot mom's nobody's fool

Aug 4
Little Boy/Girl Found

What joy, what bliss, what big relief!
The marmot kits are once more 3.
Is this a mother's normal stress,
or something clearly wrong with me
that I should spend my sleeping hours
sick-worrying about one kit?
The news is bleak, the daily showers
weak, most days, and now Don's hit
the Post Office—mail's running slow—
so all my missives may not go
to greet my loved ones far and near.
And from my lancer I'll not hear,
so carry on and work my best.
Tomorrow I shall take my rest.

Aug 5
Prehistoric Communists

My friends lost power in the storm,
while here it's dry and mostly warm,
though now and then I whiff the fall
and hope I get to stay for all
the aspens turning, flaming bright!
I watch a show about a site

in Turkey where we seem to find
a change in humans' state of mind:
11,000 years before,
our ancestors began to store
some food stuffs, which they also shared,
and that's the point at which they dared
believe they triumphed over beasts,
thus carved below, in bass relief,
the heads of "gods" in human guise.
We may have been a whit less wise,
but somehow found "cooperate"
would boost our clan's survival rate.
And so I see the coming shift
in paradigm will heal the rift
between such nations, as we've built
a global village — free from guilt.
For war was once dismissed as waste
and now there's call for greater haste
to quick evolve and dance as one —
first Trumps must go, so gods can come.

Aug 6
It's the Ballots, Stupid

I mailed more lovenotes to the world
and from my lancer got the news
the NRA would now be sued.
Today, I see the flag unfurled
above the Post Office betrays
the dirty game the Trumpster plays,
to throw a monkeywrench therein,
derail the ballots not for him.

While Putin wrings his hands and grins,
the New York D.A. churns and spins
out reams of docs from Deutschebank,
another sign Trumpland should tank.
But kill the mail? This can't be done!
(Sounds like Putin's having fun.)

Aug 7
Have They Emigrated?

No marmot greeted us today,
though skies were blue and winds were low;
all hell is breaking out below,
but five fat alpine squirrels know
our reign as good guys drawing close,
to end with fascists' blackgloved fists,
not melting pot, our global wish.
Intelligence is what we lack.
Our marmots better know than we
how to transcend their history.

Aug 8
Going Greek

I watch a 3-part doc about the Greeks:
how democracy's ideals
and fragile, egalitarian appeals
break civilizations, like our meek
democracy that drips from lips.
Again, dark ages, must eclipse
science-open-minded times,

beget forgetting, as a plague
of marble left in rain now slimes
the monuments, enclouded, vague...
what once shone clear becomes a mess
as ignorance undoes progress.

O marmot why hath thou forsaken me?
Two days now, not emerging for our break;
I miss them as the Greeks once missed their
good Socrates, who kept their minds awake.

I felt a touch of plague suggest today
my time here may be shorter than I'd choose,
or maybe it's a cold and not the way
to go out Greek, my sober mind to lose.

Aug 9
Doesn't Everybody Think They Have It?

Could be a minor cold, or maybe this
is where our subtle Covid takes its turn:
confusing victims — think they're on the mend...

I know no more today than days before.
A lonely 'munk — a chip of a thing,
much smaller than our eastern type —
with her I share my mountain lunchbreak now.

Fire that had swept its smoke this way
had lasted, so it seems, a single day;
flux and insecurity for all,
except my chipmunk who enjoys our crumbs...

I hope civilization *doesn't* fall,
a savior and Her minions quickly comes.

Aug 10
Still Worried

Feeling weirdly sick then well—
who has Covid? Who can tell...
Got a headache working hard,
rested and it seemed unmarred.
No more marmots, only sky.
The postal system goes bye-bye.
The tyrant seeks to hold his power.
We all grow weaker by the hour.
Who needs Covid to take down
this ruined nation or its clown?

Aug 11
Enter Harris

The bf and I agree,
Kamala was Joe's best bet.
How they'll both fair we'll soon see,
but Don has not attacked them yet.
I doubt he's got much ammo left;
we've seen his hand and get his drift.
The Putin whispering goes on,
but Putin can't protect poor Don,
who may just take his funds and run—
to watch his fat rump go—what fun!

Aug 12
Glad You Missed This, Mom and Dad

My parents, had they lived, could now
have 70 wed years to boast.
I'm glad they're in their graves, a vow
could not endure the hell that most
old folks are facing nowadays;
they gave their youths to fight the ways
of Hitler and his fascist friends,
but now they're gone, and nothing ends,
as history must cycle 'round...
So glad you both are in the ground.

Aug 13
We Are Belarus Now

Agony in Belarus:
the soviets resemble us.
Our protesters are disappeared,
our autocrat acts worse than weird,
revealing all his tactics now,
as if he knows precisely how
our people will react to him.

I think his chance is growing slim
to pull off such a brutal coup,
forgetting we're the people who
hold all the pursestrings of the day.

Our billionaires won't want to play;
the crush of freedoms hurts our banks,

economy more deeply tanks
if Trump prevails—we can't afford
to have the voter numb and bored.

Aug 14
Forest Fires Intensify

Fire on the mountains:
smoke makes peaks in sky.
Will we work tomorrow?
Will we breathe tonight?
A coyote(?) yelps and yelps behind
my room in dark distress.
The yelping stops so I can sleep,
no vigil left to keep.
This nation's such a mess.

I pray along with millions for
the many Covid sufferers,
alone and scared and smothering.
I dream of days when mothering—
the instinct to take care—
was all my mind was bothering.

Aug 15
Frontline Service Work: Like Death and Taxes

I early rise and scope the grounds
looking for a corpse,
but what was yelping left no trace:
relief and then remorse.

I have to go to work, for smoke
had cleared and we are sent
again way up the mountain road,
on profits most intent.
I hawk those tchotchkes hard for pay
and go at last to bed aware
the smoke had threatened us — no way,
did any bosses seem to care.
The news reminds me that now all
are risking more each Covid day,
to go to work or school, or just
to go outside to romp and play.

Aug 16
Wicked Wildfires

Again the morning reeked of smoke;
I'd kept the windows sealed all night.
The a/c made me extra cool
and now, without a frown or fight,
we bused it up and worked until
some young staffers grew quite ill.
The boss was called and down we sped,
despite a loss, a shallow till..

Again, I'm keeping out of woods
and jog past fields aflame nearby,
hoping for a change of wind,
knowing only crazy I
can give this fire a silly spin
of bosses lost in choking haze...

I hope they cancel work next morn
and give me four smoke-filled off-days.

Aug 17
This DNC Looks Almost Worth Watching!

First all-virtual D.N.C.
Shared a bit with the boyfriend — he
may or may not stick it out,
but I will watch it all. No doubt
the corn goes on, balloons may fall,
but I'll embrace it, corn and all,
for Hope is hanging in the air
like all the forest smoke out there.
They sent us home again today.
We lost some hours, gained more play;
and now I'll sleep in hope and dream
we bust this autocratic scheme.

Aug 18
Stickin' With Joe and Mamala

Ahhhh, a day cut short by fire,
I guess I'll have to just retire
into my den and watch the news.
The D.N.C. will soon amuse
and stimulate. I hope they watch:
those non-voters who still could scotch
this clear-cut choice by staying home.
I see that far as one may roam
throughout this vast great land we call

"America" she could hard fall
and crash like empires into dust...
Vote I will and vote we must!

Aug 19
Trumpeting Down the Beast

Obama calls out Trump, the black
figure who would take us back
before the Dark Age if he could.
Obama gave it hard and good,
while Gabby Giffords played French horn,
Liz Warren and each Clinton warned,
then out came Harris to go warm;
she may be tough, but can be harmed,
as Qanon, like Waco cult,
goes rabid to attack adult
responses to reality,
for they a Trump Messiah see
assuring them election heist
with mark of beast — The Antichrist!

Aug 20
Fiery Finale in Wilmington Parking Lot

Love, hope, light
and a bit of stern chastisement
from the reformed stutterer:
a gaffless delivery
for the second Irish Catholic
who might make herstory.

Shades of JFK's short reign,
but short is good,
8 years too long.
Let's keep up the acceleration,
clean up even quicker than the last
four times selfish Repubs pissed on this nation.

PS Fireworks much, much better than balloons!

Aug 21
Dream of the Deadly Red Bear

The Postmaster General lies through his teeth.
Smoke covers peaks and new valleys beneath.
Charlie the Marmot seems now all alone;
have kids and their mother all up and flown?
The flowers are few but the aspens still green.
There's sadness in smoke as it sullies the scene...
The boyfriend's attentive, our politics bind.
I dream of a Red Bear with murder in mind;
I pant and cry out, but my sleep is too sound.
One day smoke will clear and we'll vote one
more round.

Aug 22
On Top of Ol' Smoky

Ash and smoke are thickening;
my coworkers are sickening.
We sent one home at noon — no wonder.
A lone mule deer roams the tundra.

____

We sight a bull moose from our bus.
Tourists, few, still come to us
to click at mountains barely visible,
coughing on the smoke—it's risible!
There's poison in the atmosphere;
what the heck are we all doing here?

Aug 23
They Are Animate

The animals survive the smoke:
a bull moose stands in willowed turf,
ptarmigans beside our bus,
then at the tundra's top a pause
for a marmot clan to cross
(could this be Charlie's—likely not).
I wish our crew could fare as well;
we sent down 2 again today.
I wore my new N95
and meditated all my stay,
counting tourists coming in,
pausing only to greet them,
make sure each sported Covid mask—
(door-clicker's now my favorite task).
A seven hour mantra chant:
"I'm never separated from enlightenment;
I'm never alienated from the awakened place..."
At least I didn't fall asleep.
Now crowds are thinner than July.
I end tonight with nature films,
but no word from that special guy.

Aug 24
Our Herd is Thinning

A better day.
The clouds squeezed out
a drop or two.
The boss was sad
and squeezed out but a tear or two,
when told more workers plan to quit.
The young and restless here feel trapped
upon a peak, not valued and
neglected;
so she came to work
beside us for the first time since
the smoke choked out a few of us,
as if her bossly presence cheered.

And though some couples here found love,
none sees a future, no cash cow,
so move along—the boss may fear
we may not last the season now.

I still glimpse elk and sheep and vow
to watch the aspens mimic flame,
September live up to its fame.
I'll cease to play the peon's game
when snows come in the fall.

Aug 25
Animals!

A hundred elk crossed our commute
down from the peak—it wasn't cute,
the way the tourists crowded in.
We rooted for the elk and kin
to kick one in the camera phone.
Why can't they leave the beasts alone?

And miracle of morning here:
Charlie's brood is back—the dear
young marmot ran past our rear door;
one may have snuck into the store...
I hope they don't get crazy now
that they run free, and figure how
to live off humans—what a shame—
but glad to see them, just the same!

Aug 26
Watching RNC, Nose Held

The RNC lies thick as smoke;
their plans for theft are not a joke.
They cannot win, so will cheat hard.
They spread untruths like rancid lard.
I force myself to watch again,
if just to text the boyfriend when
he sends me tweets from pundits, who
say a clever thing or two,
but how disgusting, very sad,
when speakers used the time they had

to con those voters not too bright.
At last I took a walk; the sight
of smokeless hills restored my hope
that staying here I'm not a dope,
though others fly and bosses rail.
I'm grateful I don't think I'll fail
to stick it out and see what gives.
If Trump is dumped and justice lives,
if athletes say they'll stop the game,
I doubt this fall won't be the same
as other years, when speakers say
those patriotic give-aways
that try to tell us all is good.
Black players strike? I think they should.

Aug 27
More Than One Deadly Storm

A hurricane adds to the mix
of 2020's devil tricks.
The Trumpster says he wants to test
Joe now for drugs — he does his best
to show his hand and thus his fears;
Don's felt inadequate for years.
This feint reveals he can't debate,
but vowed he would. Now it's too late
to find a way to back out of
those verbal jousts we've come to love.
This RNC will be forgot;
when Trump takes stage and airs the rot
he knows that Joe will lance like boils...
They use the protesters as foils

to terrorize suburbanites,
who think the burbs belong to whites,
but few are left who haven't seen
the real domestic threat has been
white terrorists, like this new kid,
whose motives were not even hid,
when into combat-mode he slipped
and through a crowd his AR ripped.
I hope we show up who's to blame
for rioting done in the name
of justice-seekers, peaceful, who
better call to me and you
to name the rogues the camera sees:
MAGAs—Nazi wannabes.

Aug 28
That Feel of Fall in the Air

Changing seasons is everything to us animals:
so far, the aspens haven't yellowed,
the elk have not begun their rut,
but a family of bighorn sheep
posed for us on our commute.
Baby marmot poop is evident
behind the store and miracle
of miracles it rained today!
Which meant store windows must stay sealed
for weather, keeping Covid thick,
as with the prez's minions, who
seem locked in death cults, lemmings all...
As Luna waxes up tonight,
I get more pings that mean fat texts:

that he and they received my mail
sent weeks ago. The sabotaged
post office didn't quite defeat
my mission to connect with friends
across this messy continent —
they all wrote back! I am content!

Aug 29
Standing Guard at 12,000 Feet

I man the door, the tourists flow,
though traffic in our store grows slow.
I listen to the news all night:
it's clear we're heading for a fight
against the Russian lies and plot.
I hope the public's finally got
a bit of sense and can discern
truth from lies — hope now they'll learn,
or fade away in Russian style,
subjects soon of Putin's guile,
who poisons his opponents to
show Donald what *he*'s s'posed to do
to Biden, if he's worth his stripe;
though I say Don's no violent type —
a coward, as most bullies are.
I doubt the Russian plot goes far.
But just in case, I watch the door;
there's much more monkeybiz in store...

The moon grows fat.
Black Panther dies.
"Black Lives Matter" limns a mask.

Aug 30
Hyperplasia

The winds push cold,
the boss has told:
"Lock your windows
bears are feasting."
I lock mine;
I crave fresh air.
There was a rainbow
hanging where
our bus drove through;
it lasted long...
It glowed for hope.
I hope I'm wrong;
now Don's wet dream
will sure ensue:
a white militiaman — it's true —
becomes a martyr, Portland's own.
Like hungry bears, they come alone
and in their trucks to menace all
who want to sleep in peace. I fall
off dreaming of marauding bears
who've got us by the curly hairs...

Aug 31
Winter In the Air

A dark day:
I ate lunch outside the store
until the sleet drove me back in;
the wind howled worse,
the rain slashed through.
We splashed across a puddle or two.
I felt the summer giving up;
enjoyed alone a soothing cup
of chicken broth with veggies now.
I'll sleep with windows shut to howl
of winds and rains and dream again
of red bears morphing into men.

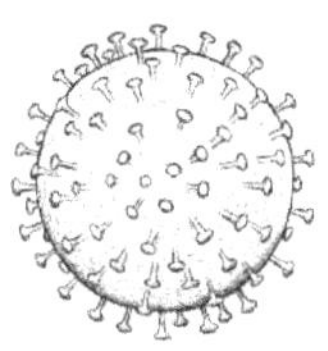

Sep 1
First Dusting!

Glory be! It snowed last night;
the frosted tundra fields delight.
We relished skies as blue as eyes,
a moon now stark in night undark,
and Don's Kenosha trip's a bust;
his eyes are skies we must not trust.
I hope black men recall Jake Blake
when they their mail-in ballots take
in hand and vote the saner way.
So much depends on them today.

Sep 2
You May Say I'm A Dreamer

I hike alone, the weather fine,
see flowers bloom, clean skies sublime
and try to think of days ahead
when only Trumpsters will be dead
from spreading virus as they say:
"If I die I die."   While I, today,
think of that lancer as I hike,
miss my neighbors and my bike
awaiting me back home. I know

I've made some money here and so
am grateful all's gone well so far.
I knew I might not see my car,
my children, or my lancer more
for working in a Covid-store,
but just today I feel as well
as ever. Hiking here is swell.
I climbed a rock outcropping to
pretend it was a mountain...
You may say I am a dreamer,
but I'm not alone, alone.
My lancer answers as I walk:
he too would like me home.

Sep 3
More Euphemisms Than Elk Today

When I taught in the ghettos, hungry teens
sucked their thumbs in class for hunger pangs.
The phrase "food insecurity" would not
have crossed my mind, instead I bought
them healthy snacks. Our addled nation
denies all want, like drunken
rabbits scared of our shadows.
Hungry kids will cry
for food here too, as parents wail
for lack of funds, while billionaires
dance on our heads. "Eat the Rich"
occurs to me, the bumper sticker
I would see in Covid times,
for many starve while others gorge
and not a word with hunger rhymes.

Sep 4
All Work is Noble

I work hard days stocking tees
and mugs and magnets for the masses
'neath skies still blue with gentle breeze;
hard to recall the world of asses.
Reporters tell of Donald's thugs,
how they stick with him like glue,
and everyone is wondering if
the military will prove true:
speak out in rage at Don's offense
and come to citizens' defense.

Sep 5
Drilling Through the Earth

I think of our brethren workers:
Who blows glass moose ornaments all day?
Who sews sweatshirts dawn 'til dusk?
Our Chinese siblings, desperate,
with no hope to end dictatorship.
Our fate looms larger as we trend
the Asian way, as masked as they,
and hear *our* autocrat decry
the Chinese enemy, (embraced
by Don's own evil family ties),
while Russia's czar now breathes on us
his poisoned breath, more stifling
than all this forest fire smoke
encroaching on our place of work.
A new uprising of the chained

workers, who would one day burn
their factories and run off free?
Chinese workers, come to me...

Sep 6
Laborers Rest

Fire closed the road today.
Home by 4, I now could play:
found a river path that took
me ten miles 'round — the air stayed good.
Now we wait for early snow,
as I and crew will not yet know
exactly when our work resumes.
"Thursday" is what one assumes...

Meanwhile, this Labor Day I'll rest,
watch the news and hope to test
Biden-Harris on the road
facing down Don's feeble goad.
They need to run like forest fires
igniting voters, blasting liars,
kick major ass election day.
(By then I'll be far, far away
from Colorado where they vote
effectively: all states take note!)

Sep 7

An Ode to the Cellular

I wasn't meant to holiday
but work, though smoke keeps us away
from mountain and its tourist store.
I walk the valley hoping for
a snowy night, though on this day
it's hazy, warm, and so I stay
closer to "home" and catch up with
my loved ones by the phone I have
always with me nowadays.
Who can remember when we stayed
in touch by letter, phones in halls
and made a whole lot fewer calls
long distance, let alone abroad?
I'm glad my kith and kin are stored
in places safe and sane compared
to many in these states now scared
to open windows on thick smoke.
The western fire's nobody's joke
and ours is still a minor rut
not likely to disturb me. How
I rue the passing summer! but
am grateful I've escaped it now,
by coming to this Rocky Park,
as free and flown as any lark.

Sep 8-10
September Snowdays

All Monday a childish vigil kept;
slowly Tuesday morning it began:
a gentle fall, a bit of breeze,
but no roaring blizzard came.
I walked in it to photograph
the summer flowers tufted with
white fluff in slow-increasing piles.
I walked a couple flurried miles
with rosy cheeks and happy face,
the firesmoke not besmudging space,
nor in my breath, all tingly with
incoming crystals, tangled with
the Ponderosa pine and sage...
I never want to turn this page.

The next day icicles fringed 'round,
the snow increased to maybe 6
inches. I traipsed white ground
with plastic bags for boots again
and caught among the new delights
a shot of elk bucks sitting down
side by side as if aware
their presence made a picture there:
symmetrical, their antlers matched.
I'd seen this pair, I do believe,
my first day here, and off and on...
two brothers? Surely not in rut,
and peaceful as a Christmas card.

I took the roads; it wasn't hard
to find much pleasure in the day,
though now the snow must melt away.

Day three: the melt, the smell of
spring, with mud and pine and river rush.
I walked to town to exercise
my right to tourist traps without
the tourists on abandoned streets,
where crowds so recently packed in.
I toured the Stanley on its hill
and photographed its steamer car,
its ancient Otis elevator,
handsome rooms and waterfall
behind a patio warm lit
with antique lightbulbs strung 'meath red
umbrellas, yet I didn't sit
in comfy couches under these,
but forged along the river where
I find the soul of Estes Park:
its 1913 cinema, its
five and dime, its quaint repose,
settling in for major snows.

I sauntered "home" to listen to
the dripping icicles and roofs
as clumps of snow land with a thud
outside my window on the mud.
This would be spring if not for here,
where Monday, on this awful year,
the temperature fell so steep
from 90 — where the natives sleep
in airconditioning — to snow...

____

Wild fires aren't extinguished though.
I sense the rangers are correct:
the pavement here still won't connect
with all the mountain road we need
to get to work, and so I cede
my time to self—no money earned.
My friend comes next week when,
we hear, it should be 70 again
with summer skies and time to mend
the damage done by fire and ice.
I'm happy—Colorado's nice!

Sep 11
New 9-11s

A sad, sad day:
Phoenix, Oregon in ashes—
will she rise?
Rote speeches and memoria ring hollow;
there's so much more to mourn today.
Finally, a whistleblower stands:
brave gal defects from Durham's sham research.
There's always hope we'll liberate ourselves...
Yet on my walk, the flag at half-mast boasts
a yardful of Trump/Pence signs, where
some insistently insist Covid's a hoax
and will not die in time,
though in a righteous universe they should,
for they believe our tax bucks must not save
the Westcoast, or the cities, or the poor
and so I wish them toward an early grave.
We need to bury all this tragic gore.

Sep 12
Still Not Able to Work Atop the Mountain Due
to Park Road Closures

Weather-induced vacay — oh no?
Spent time out in the sun, shirt free,
spooked 3 coyotes — Go! Go! Go!
An elegant elk bachelor looked at me —
(wrong species). Watched some fine TV,
reminded how it's good to see
there's beauty in the wild and art.
The world still cries, but I have heart.
Now lancer's loyal, by my side.
I hope I'll sooner take that ride
back to Denver, fly straight home,
see my peeps, no more to roam.

Sep 13
Finally, They Plow Through to Our Store

I manned the door
at the mountain store
the maskers most compliant,
but to ignore
the starving poor
would take an amoral giant.
So fat are they
that come to play
and buy our tourist favors,
I get an itch
to eat these rich
in all their sundry flavors.

Sep 14
Go Get 'Im Joe!

Don denying climate change
becomes a meme and prompts Old Joe
to coin the "Climate Arsonist"
label for our dictator.
While Vindman tells his plaintive truth
and Stone's case gets a second look,
the P.O. sends out bullshit mail
misinforming voters state by state,
plotting to deliver ballots late.
If only we'd kept civics class
essential to curricula...
We're hoisted on our own petard
"Ignorance" carried on a card —
it suits us well —
a brand we'll now all take to Hell.

Sep 15
Welcome Friend!

My friend arrives to pitch her tent
just down the road from me.
I bring us supper to eat beside
a hooting owl in nearby tree.
The elk press 'round;
the sky is blank,
I doubt we'll see one single star.
She's the friend I have to thank
for *my* being where *we* now are.

Sep 16
Two Brave Dames Kayaking in Grand Lake

We cruised the length of Trail Ridge Road,
then hit the lake to paddle some.
I sat in sun and watched her boat,
so glad she'd had the grace to come.

One plucky dame from HHS
jumps the Trumptrain to confess:
Don's a rogue who can't be moved
and Pence disowns her—such a mess!
She makes a Biden ad and shoves
the press on in their search for quotes
(as I am jotting down such notes)
to damn the Covid team's ineptitude.
We greet her with a nod of gratitude.

Sep 17
Friendship Brings New Hope

Our second day we traipsed some more
in sun and aspens turning gold.
I fear my friend's low back got sore,
but there were wonders to behold.
We ended our last night with food
served en plein air by rushing stream.

I faced the news with healthy stare
and turned to pillow, thus to dream
that maybe we'll survive this year;
this storm will pass, the air will clear,

the country turn out to elect
a team that treats us with respect.

Sep 18
R.I.P. R.B.G.

She died on Roshashana,
deciding to heed the call;
her ancestors awaited.
She turned her frail back just once
on the people she'd served so stubbornly,
had earned the title RBG.
Now paper lanterns grace Court grounds,
mourners sing "Amazing Grace,"
not a sweeter, sadder sound
resounds throughout this broken place,
where now the conversation turns
from Covid back to human rights.
46 horrific days
and many more nightmarish nights...

Sep 19
Enjoying Catered Meals As If At Ruth's Wake

The press is still digesting truth,
as I digest fine takeout borne
of Sysco's truck colliding with
our eatery dismantling
its fragile electricity.

I work too hard to think too much,
but sadder now as Ginsburg's gone
and power grabs go on and on.
Though Dems have won the seven last
presidencies by total vote,
this ain't no true democracy
and empires die upon this note.

Sep 20
No Time Wasted In Court-packing

200,000 dead from Covid now.
The power-greedy Trumpsters vow
to tip the courts 'til kingdom come,
which will come sooner as we run
from rule by our majority
to Putin-poisoned tyranny.
When Donald dies, as Hitler did,
we'll view the messy world he hid
inside his rolls of putrid fat.
If I'm alive I'll roll in that!

Sep 21
Equinox of Flu

Summer ends a lovely day:
no smoke, no snow, but now the flu
(or could be Covid?) hits the crew.
Our supervisor, worked to ruin,
sports circles under sunken eyes.
I donate my emergency

can of chicken soup (small gift),
for tomorrow we work double-shift
to inventory all our stock,
no overtime, just punching clock.
The lancer sends — at last — a note.
(I fear the tickle in my throat...)
The world's a tilt, the country shamed;
the Prez a high court justice named:
a hard-right woman to replace
dear RBG — such a disgrace!

Sep 22

Corporate Mucky-mucks Come To Kill Us

Inventory day: we take the tchotchkes' rolls.
10 corporate helpers sent, diss Covid protocols.
Trapped with maskless strangers,
I calculate the dangers,
distracted from my counting
by all the microbes mounting.
I say a prayer and hope,
I'm not another dope
who congregates inside
with folks who won't abide
by simple rule of mask.

We complete the thankless task
by eleven o'clock dark.
We exit down the park,
steep mountain road by moon.
I'm in my bed too soon.
It's hard to sleep when wired

for being overtired.
My showdown of the year.
I'll soon be out of here,
but escaping Covid-free
is all I want for me.

Sep 23
Ditty of Pity

The GOP now loves its dictatorship.
Watch all its morals slip;
tank the ol' stately ship.
Now it's clear we've got no good leadership.
Step aside for their fascist tribe.

Sep 24
Self-preservation on the Reservation

Bought myself some remedies
for all the symptoms of disease
I fear I'm coming down with now,
but rest is due me and somehow
by end of day I feel okay.
I may just squeak out virus-free.
I took a hike,
did what I like,
and took care of this worker bee.

Sep 25
RGB's Beautiful Service Brings Tears

I talk incessant politics
with friends far-flung and document
this momentous time of tears and fears,
while our First Jew now lies in state
with Hebrew songs through holy days.
It seemed so ancient in the ways
it moved me and so many more...

while Don was shamed and quickly swore
he'd pack the court and overturn
a generation's good reforms,
thus fire up the Biden base.
I hope we march all o'er the place
to keep our healthcare, women's rights
and so much more — we have more fights
to take to streets and ballot box
and note the quickly ticking clocks
running down to end this year
and pray we'll come through free and clear.

Sep 26
Unmasked Tourist Troubles

Hi-ho and back to work;
at the door I face the jerks
who try to sneak inside unmasked.
Granted, it's a thankless task
for which I'm paid a pittance, while
I had to sign a waiver-style

doc that swears I'll never sue
this company, no matter who
gives me Covid on the job.
No one would miss me here, I sob...

Sep 27
The Gray Lady Gets the Goods!

At last the NYT scores big:
tax returns for the Orange Pig.
Now Biden has more ammo for
Tuesday's debate, it looks that sure
he'll hit Don hard — let's hope he cracks —
the country can't take more hard whacks.

Sep 28
Do *You* Pay More Than the Prez?

750! Now we know!
Don's tax reveal is helping Joe.
Like mushrooms, new sharp ads appear
highlighting all injustice here:
a schoolteacher and fireman pay
much more than Trump and every day
workers die to serve our sick,
while Don would turn Supreme Court trick
to pull out healthcare from us all.
This issue also means the fall
of sick Repubs who will not spend
a buck to help recession end,

relieve the hunger of our poor,
or fight disease to ope the door
of school, or restaurant, or biz
that struggles, even more than his.
Oh Donny's up against the wall
in debt. Time for another call
to Putin, who must wish he had
a better son. A brutal dad
might kill his hapless progeny
no more of use — thus set us free.

Sep 29
Don's Despicable Debate Debut

Debate night! What a shock and blow
to every standing norm we know.
He will not play, so busts the game.
We'll build new laws in Donald's name
to strictly limit power of prez.
It's clear now, as this tyrant says:
he'll sic his Proud Boys on our polls
and then our cities. All those tolls
will end Republicans for good.
A rabid dog is shot, or should
be put down to protect the town.
No,Trump's more rabid! I turn down
the sound on all his interruptions.
Joe deflects these rude eruptions,
turning to the camera to
directly talk to me and you.
He has some plans,
he ain't no rad,

he can command
and Dems are glad
the victory tonight is clear
Biden wins — Don's outa here!

Sep 30
The War is On

Auden wrote "September 1939"
some 81 long years ago;
September 2020 ends
with a poet on TV news show,
for only poets can decry
such tragedy that you and I
must face with stark acceptance, for
here comes that juggernaut of war
that rolls across a landscape as
a forest fire and yet has
a chance of being stopped en route,
though someone's bound to slash or shoot...
So ring the churchbells, ride through night!
Shout the warning, call to fight!
Confrontation has begun.
The fascists think it's one and done,
but vicious as their presence seems,
complete with anguished women's screams,
and though we've entered past belief
those realms of endless pain and grief
where blackboots marched by night in rain
on cobblestones or tough terrain,
where now the asphalt smooths the way —
those marching boots are heard today.

____

Some poets try to capture what
Auden penned so well then, but
today we can't be too prepared —
of Trump's white army, folks are scared.
Our hope remains with soldiers who
have pledged to fight for me and you.

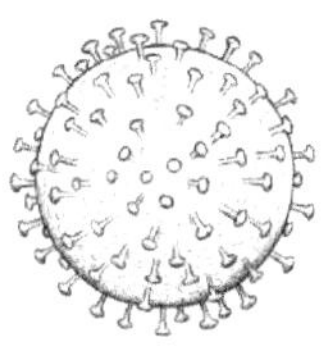

Oct 1
Will Putin Even Need His Poison?

It seems that Biden gained big bucks;
now that it's clear our Donald trucks
with violent blackboots. Putin's minions,
playing to the lout's opinions.
That White makes right still might,
prove it's Vlad who wants race fight,
but Don's indebted to him so,
the day he loses, Don must know
his hamburger's no longer safe.
Sly Vlad don't want him losing faith
in Daddy's promise to protect
the secrets saving Donny's neck.
The frightened pig is squealing now,
but Whitepigs love him anyhow
and plan to fight the martyr's cause,
though lost. I doubt they'd ever pause
and think about this hopeless battle.
Still, they manage now to rattle
nerves across this anxious land.
This isn't quite what Putin planned;
but Vlad is patient and can wait
long past the Trumpster's Bigot-gate,
attack again when things are back
to normal, so I hope we whack

deplorables back into holes
and keep intact our voter rolls.

Late Breaking News:

Corona virus hits Hope Hicks:
the WH in a bigger fix.
Will Don go on to Michigan,
spew virus on his troops again?

Later Breaking News:

(It's still October 1 out West.)
Now Trump and wife show Covid test
as positive as failing state
of health — I hope — *this* news is great!

Oct 2
Hitler at Walter Reed

To quote the lancer:
"Incompetency is Trump's brand."
I'm sure this campaign hasn't gone as planned.
Another friend thinks it's a dirty trick:
"Trump's only faking that he's sick."
We may not know, the docs won't tell
the body politic if he's sick or well.
He tweets out "LOVE!!!"
to all his crazy fans.
We doubt he'll debate again. His plans
for rallies cancel everywhere;
true devotees likely wouldn't care,

but will they vote? Discouraged as they'll be
as Dear Leader hides in hospital... We'll see
no nasty ads from decent Biden team,
while Trump attacks go on. It seems
a host of Don's Repubs are taking ill.
Will they stay out of hearings on the Hill?
Maybe this will end well for the Dems.
On White House docs this country now
depends.

Oct 3

Vote You Youngsters Vote!

This evening on the ride back in the van,
a couple coworkers were chatting up a storm.
I held off longer than I often can,
but had to jump into the verbal swarm.
It seems a lot of hate expressed for Trump
exists among the service worker class.
I said if he's a Prez you want to dump
you must get up and vote or kiss your ass
goodbye, for now it takes a bit of wit
to conjure what a second term would bring.
To think was not exactly what they're taught,
but somehow they'd got hold of this one thing:
"Trump's bad" and we should "get his family
out."
"Well," says I, "that's what voting's all about."
Let's see if angry youth turns out this year.
There's nothing that'd bring old Dems more
cheer.

Oct 4
Golden Leaves in Gray Smoke

The aspenglow shone through the smoke.
Trump's Covid case still not a joke;
he risks the lives of others, so
around the block he goes to show
the minions honking outside Reed
he thinks they're swell and has a need
to drink their love as if their blood.
Some comment Prez car ride's not good.
More thousands die on Trump's new show...
Like aspen leaves — will he soon go?

Oct 5
Drawing the Mountains in My Mind

"The mountains are calling and I must go..."
John Muir tells us this, I know.
I ride the bus and meditate
upon the lines that illustrate
this landscape vast and varying.

Now images I'm marrying
with human bodies: women lie
on backs with breasts askew and high,
topped with rock nipples rippled, dark.
Forgetting this is man's own park
with roads crisscrossing, still I see
the tawny tundra rolling free
to end in pubic juniper.
Her eyes, the glacial lakes that pool

in every socket underneath
the high snowfields that year-round wreath
these peaks which point as praying hands.
The meadows down below are strands
from photos yellowing with age;
the aspen blonds in profile stage
female faces raised to sky.

I'll soon bid this wild place goodbye
and though I've known so little of
these mountains I can say I love
the lines they draw, the figures here
that I, as well as Muir, held dear.

(Yet soon as I get my crude portrait just so,
bus rounds a bend: she becomes a Picasso.)

Oct 6
Work Bus Traded for Cramped Vans, Oh My!

Two girls cry Covid wolf today
just before we drive away
in vans now packed; I cringe beside
the tiny window opened wide
as it will go. Alone I'm masked;
I've never shown my frown and asked
these clowns to mask themselves for me.
If I get home now Covid-free
I'll gladly say a thousand prayers
for all those suffering the cares
of workers, who must listen to
their peers cry "Covid" as if "Boo!"

____

(It seems they'd been out partying
so now, hungover, "Covid" sing.)
We glare and gasp and cross our chest,
but wearing masks would serve us best,
though bosses claim work "bubbles" work —
I fear each careless vector-jerk.

Oct 7
VP at De-Bates Hotel

The fly — well trained by Dems, no doubt —
helped "Mamala" achieve her rout.
Pence looked morose with forehead sweat;
then came the fly — it's a safe bet
none will recall the words of Mike,
but fly-memes get ten million likes.
For two whole minutes it took charge,
trotting Mike's white hair at large
and countered his attempts to mute
his opponent — none thought cute
to watch a white man shush and rule
a brilliant black AG. The fool
was playing hard to one sick viewer;
now Trump's female voters fewer
than before the Pence-poor show.
Is this surprising? Oh *hell* no!

Oct 8
Gov. Whitmer Kidnapping Plot Revealed

Now it's revealed some white-nat fools
planned kidnapping and blowings up
in Michigan — which surely cools
Don's rhetoric and fills the cup
of Biden's independents, who
see chaos and a chance for change...
Meanwhile, our Prez has gone coo-coo:
Pelosi says she'll now arrange
a hearing re the 25th
that all know will go nowhere, yet
it gets at the election's pith:
Don's nutz and Joe's a certain bet.

Oct 9
Don Stuck "Home" Still Sick Yet Dangerous

Dear Leader will conduct campaign
rallies from the White House, while
in Michigan the cops disdain
the laws and love militiamen
so well we'll see more actions vile,
more deaths until we've had enough,
enact new laws and take a tough
hand of justice to this lot
who flaunt each crime.
There's not much time,
but will we've got.

Oct 10
Last Commute Down the Mountain Owed to
Fires and Snows

We closed the store in the park today.
I felt a bit soft as we drove away
in silence on our last commute,
the mountains glorious en route,
though smoke rose from a dozen fires;
and now the season's work requires
we rest a day then work below
as still we prep for midnight snow...
The timing could not be more clear:
we made it to the end this year.
The tourists got their trinkets, while
the corporates got a modest pile
of profits from our enterprise,
and I believe I've now survived
a season working with a crew
that acted as if this were flu
and not a virus out to kill.
The snow will bring a peaceful chill
to slow down humans in these parts
and warm a bunch of feral hearts.

Oct 11
Prepping to Leave

I'll soon be by my patient lancer,
to wish for snow to cover over
Jersey's fields and meadows, so
upon cross country skis I'll go...

Though it would thrill my heart to see
Rocky snow drown that old store,
I'll kiss my lancer fervently,
grateful to be home the more.

Oct 12
New Justice — No Justice

Amy Coney Barrett will
be seated on the highest court
and set upon her mission 'til
all progress she has helped abort.
Now Dems will have to compensate
to keep the voters pacified,
restore democracy to make
the *majority* those who decide
what laws are passed, what judge confirmed
for years ahead through pain and death.
Rule by majority, we've learned,
is democracy and nothing less.
The next few months could horrify
the nervous and the timid who
delude themselves and glorify
this country as if no one knew
we were in shambles, as we' d sold
our souls to corpirates long ago;
democracy's worth more than gold,
as this election tells us so.
So pack the courts, I say, and soon!
Restore the justice of the many.
We who occupied the moon
can throw the poor a pretty penny!

Oct 13
Getting Ready to Trade Prairie for Swamp

My last full day in the valley where
I've lived a happy hermit's life:
I'll do my laundry now and dare
to take a hike, ignore the strife
as Dems in Congress try to prove
they care about the minions, who
are at this minute voting for
a chance at healthcare even more
needed in these Covid days,
though now is not the time to raise
the specter of a larger court.
I'll walk these mountains and cavort
with nature to restore my glee,
though Coney Barrett's face I see
on every channel — it's too much!
The woman's clearly out of touch
with what the masses want today,
but she's not going anyway.
We must stand firm and recognize
we'll have our turn to organize
a whole new set of big reforms
that best reflect the day's new norms
and in the mix I hope to see
the laws against such bigotry
as Trump has pushed into the fore;
we can't ignore it anymore.
Someday we'll thank him for this feat,
but first we'll rally to defeat
his sycophants who gave us Barrett —
we'll rebuild courts to fit their merit!

Oct 13 (addendum)
Last Walk Along the Big Thompson
(for DS)
Sunbaked Ponderosa pine,
the first thing I would smell,
now mingled in with stallion dung;
trail riders know it well.
A tinge of smoke from far-off fires,
the freshet down below:
this is Rocky Mountain land,
a haunt you once did know.

Oct 14

Homeward Bound in N95

Leaving Estes Park, the plume
of firesmoke blotted half the sky.
It seems there wasn't any room
for me to stay, so said goodbye.
The risk I took, the preps I'd made,
accepted death as one result
that lived with me and wouldn't fade,
but never did such dread insult
my eagerness to love this place:
the mountains I had never known.
And through the days of death I'd face,
I must admit I must've grown
and somehow got away with it—
N95 no perfect fit.
So, so long Rockies, park and all...
hello to East Coast friends and fall!

———————————————————

Oct 15
A Little Help

My friends took such good care of me:
I made it home with food and rest;
flowers greeted me. I see
my home survived—and all the best
weather, colored leaves and sun!
Low altitude, damp climate, meant
I braced myself to have new fun
back where my youth was mostly spent:
familiar seasons, swampy woods.
The moisture made my musty bed.
I want the world to share the goods
I bring with me inside this head
where hope remains, though I had fears—
great fears of dying far from home—
I seem to have escaped, my dears,
and vow for now I shall not roam.

Oct 16
First Things First

A rainy day, so good for rest,
my car kaput, my lancer still
not ready to so quick invest
in having me, in case I'm ill.
I walked to Walgreens, dutiful
to get my flu shot and behave
as though my life is beautiful,
as I'm still this side of the grave.

The Trumpsters' plot to kill the old,
the brown, infirm, and Dems galore.
I hope we leave them in the cold
and give them power nevermore.

Oct 17
Fall Glorious Fall!

Another day of sun and tones
so bright and gay to follow stint
of mountain greens and prairie browns,
the sunlight manages to glint
off surfaces familiar, yet,
now rediscovered with delight.
So good to see my humble pet
possessions in the autumn light.
I wish my lancer would invite
me to his outdoor fire pit,
yet if he takes his time he might
start smoldering and spark a bit.
He knows I'm here, but doesn't yet
understand I'd need a ride;
that he will come's no certain bet...
I wait, a princess, no one's bride.

Oct 18
Warming Up the Wheels

I ride my bike at river's edge.
The leaves delight, the smells bewitch.
My lancer chose his bets to hedge.

I've fallen in this yearning ditch
brought on by fall and Covid fears
that isolate me from his arms
and thus, while biking, through my tears
send him pictures, write him charms
in hopes he'll light a fire soon,
invite me to converse at least,
or meet me for a meal at noon,
or lock his eyes in staring feast...
Alas, we seem not to conjoin;
I end the day alone again,
sequestering my own shy coin—
the Covid cost to nervous men.

Oct 19
Side Effects

Still life: a day of rest,
I must admit, not my best.
That flu shot maybe made me ill?
Glad I never took a pill,
but rested, talked a lot to friends,
wrote and emailed—all depends
on attitude and patience now.
I got my car back, anyhow;
spent hundreds more to make it run
(not sure if that's what *you*'d have done).
I did, and I guess I must
keep driving it—though hard to trust
its weary parts to keep me safe.
350K miles chafe
at choking out more engine grease.

I'm cheap, I know, and will not cease
to hold on to a favorite toy...
and that reminds me of the boy
I'm waiting for — he texted — late.
Still haven't heard about a date
we'll finally meet face to face,
but I have patience — that's a grace.

Oct 20
Because I Registered My Travel With the State

State of New Jersey called to see
if I were quarantining right;
was glad I answered and could be
home as ordered, though I might
have been out driving, which I was,
and walking in the beauty-woods...
My car is running! That's becuz
I treat it well and buy it goods:
a brand new battery and stuff,
expensive though these are, and I
have money, but not near enough
to buy a car and that is why...

O glorious the colors here!
Oh loving are my local friends
and all my buds both far and near,
who keep me sane, as all depends
on patience and acceptance of
my circumstances and my flaws.
I know I've got my lancer's love
while I'm obedient to laws —

he *is* a legal-germaphobe
and so expects me to comply
with quarantines, though will not probe
me on my health—I ask not why
he hesitates to see me now,
yet texts me as he's always done.
I'm grateful he can keep a vow;
I trust he has no other one.

Oct 21
Orange and Black

The orange rain of leaves flows gently now,
the howling winds of yesterday far gone.
I take a walk through town with friends and vow
I'll stay as settled here as anyone.
The boyfriend's still in touch and still a tease;
he tells me Trump's too dumb to wag a dog.
I get upset with every new release
of news of threats and spend much time agog,
expecting, any moment, dropping bombs,
material or metaphorical.
I vision weeping children, grieving moms,
as lies rain down, not categorical,
but random as the dropping forest leaves,
a steady propaganda stream to rig
election as the Trumpster's brand deceives.
Yet, voters know no lipstick on this pig
can camouflage the evil ones' intent:
that we should be defeated in our souls.
Barack's address in Philly heaven-sent,

designed to shoot, benignly, full of holes
the DNI's suggestion than *Iran*
is hurting Trump by hacking voter rolls.
I hope each voter does all he/she can
to fight for free elections over trolls.

Oct 22
World Series of Doubt

A last debate — thank gods that's done!
Neither was a model candidate;
it's hard to say that Biden won.
Clearly, Don was not that great.
Much better was the night before
when Rays beat Dodgers 6-4;
the boyfriend wants to please old Vin,
but I want underdogs to win...
My bikeride through the wall of leaves,
out past the ponds and riverside,
was balm my thirsty soul receives,
while in the news the fires ride
into that valley I once loved
by foot and eye and pine-filled nose.
Estes Park has now been shoved
into the furnace — I suppose
it was my fortune to have seen
a Western 'scape so pristine, green.
The flames in Jersey are but hues,
while Coloradans sing the blues...
My old friend on his brand new ranch
is still untouched by wildfires there.
He wrote and showed me how he'll prance

on horseback as he learns to care
for horses, cows and real estate:
a project sure to last his life.
I'm happy we had time — he's great!
But glad I'll ne'er more be a wife...
Still waiting for the summons from
the one I love here who must know
the State now eyes my quarantine
and I am patient, still, and slow...

Oct 23
One Vote Lighter

A day of rehash of the last debate,
while Covid cases rise — it's all too late
when forty million cast an early vote.
Two soggy Friday hours I would devote
to hiking 'round the lake, stop at the bank;
for what I'd earned this summer I could thank
the Powers that have lately set ablaze
far meadows and dry hills I once would praise.
Then I, my ballot for the first time cast
by dropping in a box now bolted fast
before the town hall and its loyal cops,
to join the minions in their ballot drops...
for waiting seemed too risky lest I fall
prey to the virus hunting one and all.

Oct 24
Canvassing the Pumpkins

This morning was a day to put my feet
to work for Dem who must again compete
against a redder, southern Jersey foe,
so 'round the foreign neighborhood I'd go...
He's not my congressman, but one who needs
support, and thus I had agreed
to work today and then on Halloween
in hopes another victory he'll glean;
thus, I feel more effectual than not.
My friend and I then took a gentle trot
around the schools, which seem to be in gear,
beginning late the 2020 year.
Again I say my grace for all good timing —
my kids are grown, and I'm hellbent on
rhyming.

Oct 25
Still Hope for Underdogs

Once more, last night the ballgame must go on;
the bottom of the ninth young Tampa won!
It seemed a miracle! My lancer would
have Kershaw win this time —
I guess he should —
but I am always for a seven-game
series just as I am loathe to name
the winner in advance of any vote.
We learned the hard way last time — don't emote!
Don't say the name, don't dare predict the win!

Stay vigilant and humble—it's a sin
to go too cocky toward election day.
We only wish now Don would fade away...
We hardly care if he goes out in cuffs,
or flies the coup and hides—we'll call his bluffs
because we're all so weary and so blue;
we've gone through some of Covid, but aren't
through.
There's much more dying in the months ahead.
The Trumps survived, though many wish them
dead.
The movies and the ballgames pass the time.
The days go gray now, fading leaves sublime
as down they tumble from the shaken trees
as if to shrug off Trumps, our land's disease.

Oct 26
Masque of the Red Justice

As Amy Coney Barrett takes the court,
the white house holds another Covid fete
to roast the social programs she'll abort,
but we ain't seen the end of Barrett yet.
We'll have to watch more misery and grief,
while people suffer more and more each day
the new injustices beyond belief,
as healthcare and their rights are robbed away.
And Mitch may be around to see the end
of his arcane yet clumsy house of cards.
Though grim the reaper, we shall long contend
it's our democracy his act retards.
The sentiment, as poured into the streets,

will be so strong it cannot be recessed,
and I, too, plan to live long just to greet
the Dems' new justices, this mess redressed.
For Biden hems and haws, but many more
will clamor to restore the courts before
we go again to vote, and this be true:
in first 6 months Prez Biden can accrue,
democratic norms we *shall* restore!

Oct 27
It's All Over Now Baby Blue

Mookie scores — in six the Dodgers win,
which vindicates the boyfriend and Old Vin.
Now Barry closes stronger than Old Joe
(he is the better speaker, don't we know),
while Don goes on how virus can't be bad;
after all, a "mild case" he had.
Melania is dragged out on the trail,
while all the Dems work hard to make them fail.
Don's lawsuits mount; the high court backs them up,
but Trumpsters may be running out of luck,
as early voting seems the in thing now.
I hope we see a landslide and I vow
no matter what, I'll keep up my good fight.
The people won't go quiet into night.
They'll once again demand their right to health
and a somewhat bigger bite of richmen's wealth.
The youngsters go to vote now, as they should,
and all the pollsters indicate it's good
news for the Dems if kids turn out

(and that's not all this day was all about).
I walked with friend then bought a lot of food,
cooked, completed puzzle and made good
on promise to myself to learn to sing
"The Urge for Going" which forever brings
a smile and tear as autumn's bittersweet...
Elections, like baseball games, defeat
my womanly concern for fairness, as they show
that some must fall as others flee the snow.

Oct 28
Waiting With Borat

Today I awoke to find
not frost upon our town,
but Donald stranding loyalists
where hypothermia knocked them down.
Like a bunch of trusting tots,
who find the sing-song ravings of a charlatan
comfort to their wounded pride,
we won't see them again.
No, we won't see those who die from cold
or Covid as they worship at the Donald's feet...
They've got the urge for going
and now we'll never get to meet.
Biden chides the monster now
for Covid jealousy.
"Covid! Covid! Covid!" rants
the clown in green envy:
our virus gets more airtime
than the Prez, who only curses it
and walks away...

This, I told my lancer, was
my favorite news today.
Now my friend has me for tea and tube;
we watch *Borat* just for fun.
The lancer knows my quarantine
is over now — I'm done.
No wandering, no wondering,
I'm ready to be his,
but still I await his beckoning;
that's just the way it is...

Oct 29
Too Many Nasty Winds

Today a hurricane called "Zeta,"
latest of a lengthy string,
brought down leaves here and as great a
dump of rain, yet not one thing
was ruined here, as in the south, where
seven hurricanes have hit,
for there's an open salty mouth there
into which more storms have bit.
In Jersey, it's pre-Halloween,
the time when colored leaves are downed
by autumn rains and winds — we've seen
it every year — as comes around
election-time, where rains of lies
drive huddled masses from their homes
to streets where law and justice dies,
while there the Trumpster's army roams.
They threaten to harass the voters
at the polls if not before.

Now Russian hackers race their motors,
ripping through our cyber core;
it seems they're meant to cast new doubts on
close-call tallies so the court
will overrule protesters' shouts on
streets where Proud Boy types cavort,
brandishing their hefty rifles—
this, a hurricane to come...
The Russian hacks are merely trifles.
Listen for the rebels' drum!
They say a second civil war is
what they want to start this year.
If we're to weather such a storm, this
Trump gang's got to fail—y'hear!

Oct 30

Live and Not Zoomable

Finally—the long-awaited day:
he'll let me see him; I can only say
"Thanks gods!" You kept me healthy and I trust
you'll keep us safe together as we must
try hard to make a bubble for our bed,
and if the country fails and goes too red—
red like Putin's Russia, red like blood—
I'll keep him company and be as good
as any partner fighting side by side
to put things right. At least we'll never hide
or cower, when we know we must be brave,
and much as him I love, I'll fast abide
my commitment to this nation save.

Despite full moon, he, like a cat,
received me warily and cold,
but I was only grateful that
he let me for a brief time hold
him after talk of politics,
which all the day was rife with strife.
Don's bullies tried to stop Joe's bus;
the dueling rallies, lunatics,
attacks by cops with pepper spray,
the press corps racing to keep up,
as votes and virus records made
and all I'd done this day was pray
my lancer would be glad to see
a citizen True Blue as me.

Oct 31
My Final Door-to-door Effort

Halloween with morning sun,
I raced about to talk to one
more voter who had not turned out;
the Congressman may face a rout
if Trumpsters outvote Dems down there,
where Jersey rednecks only care
for "Freedoms" such as owning guns.
I hope they're not the winning ones...
The season's rains returned at night;
I trust the kids were treated right.
So sad they lost their costume-day,
as Covid now must take away
so many happy holidays,
impacting all in different ways.

Now even I am lonelier,
since he is close yet can't confer
the love I crave, but gives to me
a film suggestion, so I see
a moving film and bake some sweets.
One who tricks for love gets treats.

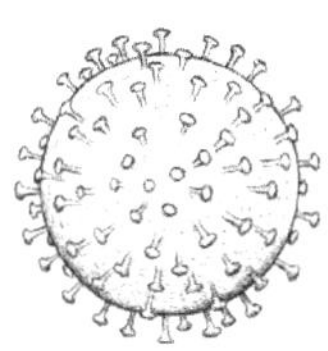

Nov 1
Two to Go

November dawns an extra hour;
I needed sleep. But not the shower
of steady rain that fell once more,
though campaigns surged upon the poor
and ignorant who must be coaxed
to vote, not fall for some Trumped hoax.
Don says today he'll claim a win
before the counting can begin.
It's clear we're in for more than one
long testy night 'fore counting's done
and gods knows what his boys will do,
while Trump himself proves to be through...
A winner who can't lose must flee.
I hope he leaves his family,
for someone from his empire must
go down in chains and eat his dust.
Don blaming doctors now for greed
is just the fuel some Dems may need
to rouse themselves in rain and snow
and vote at last for milktoast Joe.
Election innovations must be noted:
a vast majority have early-voted;
drive-up voting's proven popular,
like Biden rallies witnessed from one's car

---

where honking takes the place of shouts and
roar.
Conventions via Zoom we feared might bore
turned out to be as good as well-made flicks.
And though the Trumpsters seem to get their
kicks
imagining they live in 1950,
the Dems think innovations rather nifty.
Hard to imagine going back again,
when conventions crowded with white men
in funny hats with speeches from buffoons
ended in inevitable balloons.
I hope the Covid era makes it clear —
technology advanced a lot this year,
and people — even Trumpsters — could adapt.
Let's hope it's also written the big map
to show a blending of the red and blue —
for purple ought to be the Covid hue.

Nov 2
Fingers, Toes, Arms, Legs, Eyes Crossed

Election eve and tensions rising high,
too high for Bidenites—they're braced to cry.
I hedge my expectations, but go on
with optimism, as no contest's won
by ruing every effort, every hope.
I know with any outcome I can cope,
but that's because I'm old and wish to die
right here in this doomed land. I cry
for younger ones, who, like my son, can see
the work ahead is hard as hard can be,

with climate bearing down like one great storm,
the politics just putting off the harm
our kids must face and try to rise above.
I'd save them, but I know my earthy love
is not not enough to change the policies
that lead to poisoned skies and rising seas;
and now we wait to see if we've a chance
to start the climate-rectifying dance.
Of course, the loss of humans will go on,
as Mother sends us plagues galore and Don-
like tyrants steal the goods and hide;
but there's no hiding place–she'll slip inside.
It's Prince Prospero at his masked ball now
and ships of fools don't stay afloat, no how.

Nov 3
We Probably Won't Know Tonight

At last! At last! The fatal day is here,
though once returns come in it's not more clear...
There is no landslide. Biden hasn't solved
the situation and the hope's dissolved
that vital changes here will save this land.
I wonder how long the plebes can stand
the agonizing vote counts that go on —
who knows — for days now, weeks? And so our Don
is *not* yet vanquished, *not* drained out like pus,
and thus the slog continues — pity us!

Nov 4
Win Some — Lose Some

As if our nerves were frayed yet not enough,
getting through another vote-count day was
tough.
We lost the Senate...that was crushing and
some House seats — does this mean we're
damned
eternally by Grim-Reaper Mitch
to never scratch the ol' progressive itch,
to bring about some change long overdue?
The kids are restless — as for me and you,
we may be aging, but forever true
to causes life-long fought for, yet we knew
this could be yet another ugly fight.
I walked with friend, did puzzles, spent the
night
laughing at some mockumentaries,
trying to forget this dread disease
that's hit the body politic with all the force
of headless rider on runaway horse.

Nov 5
Hoover Days Are Here Again

Again, I barely listened to the news,
held my breath and went outside to lose
the horrid crippling dreads and near despair
that clouds the oceans, muddies up the air.
Yet, how nice to be called to come sit
a spell with ladies on a lawn,

to chat and even laugh a cautious bit,
collectively, forgetting that the dawn
will break again with votes still not secure,
Covid cases rising, no near cure,
the poor much poorer,
though the Trumpsters can't
feel an ounce of pity so they shan't
pass any legislation for relief
and things will soon go south beyond belief,
the likes of 1932 though ten times worse,
for now we add the viral rampant curse.
Well fed, I am content to go to bed
with visions of disaster in my head.
It's clear the reign of Hoover ushered in
the Roosevelt reforms that must begin
again to cast a wide, strong, lasting net
to keep us all aboard as decks get wet
and bulkheads burst and engines fail to turn
as stern descends, sails and lifeboats burn,
the cries drown out the orders, captain's last,
to go down with the ship — *he*'s steaming past
the wreck, for he is bound to get away
to torment other minions in a day
not yet known, but tilting off the level,
skewing toward the rich friends of the Devil.

Nov 6

Changing Light at Island Beach

There was a haze at the beach today;
I let my head go into it:
Fuzzing my thoughts like binoculars
malfocused,
I saw two tents on an island — no boat.
I saw a small teddy bear with hand-knit sweater,
face down in the dunes,
a child's pink shoe half-buried on the high tide
line.
Even my ritual meditation on the waves was
choppy, disjointed;
swells rushed toward me uncounted.
There was too much counting today, anyway.
Still tallying, slavishly, to eke out a slim victory
in a divided time so breached
there appears no bridge.
Yet, as I trudged beneath their fishing lines,
I tried to accept the penises thus thrust seaward:
the machismo of the Trump male,
his ginormous vehicle parked, atop deflated
tires,
a noxious whiffs of cigar smoke and the smell of
charcoal bricks in sand.
I doubt they could feel my prayers flagging on
their empty lines...
I want to make peace,
yet I can not think for all this
counting, counting, counting and waiting for the
tug.

Nov 7
For *Whom?*

Paris ringing bells for us!
The world takes one collective breath.
The win's announced mid-morning and
the people pour into the streets.
I bike to find compatriots,
but all are eating in plein air.
The speeches are just right, and then:
fireworks in a parking lot
in Wilmington! In *Wilmington* —
that empty, tragic, Bidened town!
Yet now our heads can hit our beds
and hope come sparkling down...

Nov 8
Upbeat At Last

Another Indian summer's day:
I went out in the woods to play
with others grooming garden space
for native plants where paths would trace
the landscape random, full of glee,
the children caring for a pond
they'd made for frogs and all could see
new smiles like mushrooms bulging on
sweet faces bent in outdoor play
to celebrate this brighter day.

Emails from kin in Germany
congratulating us and we

can better understand *them* now —
though saved this time — no one can vow
a lasting democratic will.
As Don's refusing to concede,
I trust he'll hold his line until
that Loser's got the balls he'll need
to face the firing squad of law,
or disappear into the maw
of Putin's hungry shark-toothed grin.
It seems there's senate seats to win
in Georgia still — more hope that way...
It's warm and sunny — time to play!

Nov 9
Covid Scare Number 9

I played too hard! Now I'm blue.
It seems I've got that Wuhan flu.
Could this low fever and these aches
be indicators? For it takes
about ten days, the length of time
since I saw him — does this mean I'm
infected from a boyfriend who,
much more than I, is scared of flu?
Oh well, the day went on and by
the evening I could see that I
exaggerated, through my fear,
a sinus infection that did clear,
so by the time I went to bed,
corona virus woes had fled.
Oh gods! How long can one sustain
this bracing for the wracking pain

of *real* corona sickness that
is really killing minions at
overcrowded hospitals?
I'm now embarrassed by false calls;
but what's a person here to think
as U.S.A, is on the brink
of sheer collapse from its denials?
I'd rather go through phantom trials...
Imagination's not a crime;
thanks gods I made it through this rhyme.

Nov 10
Hospitals Crowding Up Again

61,000 frantic souls:
flapping fish on hospice boats...
More mad counting at the polls,
those mainly-Biden mail-in votes,
the weather crazy-hot as if
all this friction-kindled fire,
the governors now frozen stiff
for coddling the infant liar.

Nov 11
Bewitchery

O to walk in rain on warm November nights,
caped figure shadowed under pumpkin lights,
smelling witches brew: fermented leaves,
pine and osage orange pungence cleaves
the sadness of the stalemate brought by fear,

not of us ghouls, but of the raging year
where pols grow sicker by the hour yet live,
a witches' curse on those who fail to give
their measly alms to ever-hungry poor,
a crowd pressed up against our bolted door.
There must be witches powerful and wise
to clear away the mildew in the guise
of brave elected men and women who
we simply ask to lead and do it true.

Nov 12
Ditat Deus!

It's 290 to 217
as Arizona's now a win;
for though most Goppers haven't seen
the light—Joe Biden *will* step in!
A few would like to give him briefs;
intelligence is threatened now,
but Don, who's settled into grief,
has stubbornly dug in. Somehow
it seems his sons are on his team,
while daughter may be softening;
perhaps the Kush has interests, too,
in Trump divorce—before we're through.
The closest ones may go to jail
and take the blame for all this death.
I doubt they'd even make their bail,
for little Trumpworld will be left.

The scams go on to bilk the boors
of money for the Trump estate,
believing he'll come back in four
years, though it will be too late
for them to earn their money back
from their beloved crook-in-chief:
a TV fraud, a grifter, hack,
it's hard to fathom their belief,
their absolute devotion to
a man who simply validates
the evil in us all, and who
sinks all ships—oh take him Fates!

Nov 13
He *Never* Will

It's Friday the 13th and yet
somehow the Prez found strength today
to address the nation—you can bet
the one big thing he didn't say
was "I concede," though he let slip
a tiny movement toward that goal,
as votes still counted clearly tip
Joe's eagle soar past Donald's hole.
Meanwhile, the bad-luck day proved true
as millions more infected now.
1,200 die each day from flu
and Dems are warning this is how
we show our weakness to the world—
not just as failed democracy.
Into chaos we've been hurled,
with 70 million more crazy

than e'er before upon this soil;
they think their grifter Prez is God!
Putin's plot we now must foil
and scrape off this annoying clod.

Nov 14
Escape from Trumplandia

Me, I pedaled through the countryside
to worship none but Nature, Holy Bride.
I lay in sun and watched the falconed clouds
far, far away from Trumpish Covid crowds...

The Million MAGA March looks like
a Trump inauguration shot:
with thinner crowds, though some would strike
some counter-protesters, though not
deadly, one was stabbed, a score
arrested, after Don drove by
at one point on his way to putt,
waved at them and winked an eye.
His gilded knife — a deeper cut,
they should know they'll get no love.
I almost pity them and yet
they carry rifles, push and shove
deny hard facts, go maskless, set
fires at demos, loot and make
the violence they would hope to pin
on Black resistors, who still take
to streets, (which hardly is a sin) —
then tell us all this news is fake.

Nov 15
Sundays at the Community Garden

I work outside in grayer skies,
(November's starting to get real),
talk with neighbors, building ties
as all of us can say we feel
exhausted by events of late,
while gardening's the common cure;
we rue the failures of the state
and hope the union will endure...
But, oh it feels so good to chat
outdoors with people just like me
and to remember where it's at:
clearing dirt around a tree,
building paths and labeling plants...
We make a place for all to play,
for one day soon Trump's sycophants
will — like the leaves — just blow away.

Nov 16
Pampered Birds

I spoke with both the kids today.
They're doing fine and all is well,
so out I rode to go the way
of rivers, and to feel the swell
of wind and sun as if the sea
(though all we have here is a lake),
the cormorants all seemed to be
begging — guess the locals take
them treats, or maybe fishermen

throw them bait. While minions starve
and thousands die, we'll know not when
a pumpkin's worth of peace we'll carve
out from the patch of angry weeds,
who clamor still for Donald's reign,
though what this country clearly needs
is cash infusion and a drain
so big and deep the swamp is cleared
and, like this crystal lake, can thrive.
Far off the path we've sorely veered
and pray our country can survive.
Another vaccine comes with hope.
Moderna says it won't require
the deep freeze that the other dope
from Pfizer must have, lest the dire
consequence of wasted cures
will haunt us as the Covid dead.
I pray long life for mine and yours,
as well children's daily bread.

Nov 17
Invite: All Right!

The lancer waxes chatty late at night;
I close my eyes to savor my delight.
The invitation: fire pit Friday eve!
It's been three weeks, my itch I'll soon relieve,
and even if he doesn't want to touch,
our firelit facetime means so very much.
Though girlfriends on the phone sustain me well,

his presence makes my untuned heartstrings
swell
to fugues as convoluted as his mind
and smiles as wide as sentiments that bind
two awkward souls who meet across a flame
to play a round of their specific game.

Nov 18
Princeton Reeks of History

I muse on George's army as I tramp
through Continental battlefields most damp,
decrying all the loss and black decay
that's come to our young nation by this day.
The Fathers never could have seen this clown
tearing their well-crafted system down
by still refusing to relinquish power
as he ransacks all departments by the hour,
firing all who serve their country with
devotion *he* would never deign to give.
(Take Krebs, the guy who kept the voting safe —
his competence the Donald's ass would chafe.)
Our Constitution badly needs reforms
to catch up with this population's norms.
I think, as on I trudge, this lovely day
and finally, while wondering what I'd say,
I find a show on Netflix perfectly
suited to this hour — you may agree —
'bout spies George Washington recruited when
he needed loyalty from certain men,
who undertook that dangerous career
and brought us through the war and out of here,

where bodies lie around me —
Princeton's tomb—
of patriots with musket balls of doom,
so I could lie abed and type this now.
Though all those ghosts are turning, I shall vow
to keep the faith democracy will win
and some new shining era soon begin...

Nov 19

My New Career: Staying Out of Hospitals

Had yearly check-up, doctor says I'm fine.
Walked some 10+ miles and spent some time
talking to my peeps both far and near,
checked the news and learned it's just as clear
that Trump's a traitor as the sky was blue,
the grasses golden and the hawk that flew
above the meadow where the sun turned gold:
the scintillating scene we'd both behold.
While millions sick in homes and ICUs,
must conjure in their sickbeds meadow views,
I traipse about in guilt I don't do more
than take care of my self and close the door
on Covid and my neighbors, who might need
some aid, when all I've got to give is greed.
I'm probably no better than the Don,
though I leas, not golf greens, tread upon.
Still, my career of being Covid-free
is taking care of more than only me.
It feels unlovely to be selfish thus,
so I write hope and prayers for all of us.

Nov 20
Pale Fire

The fire pit, stars, and slender moon,
the outdoor dining on the square,
the sense that all could end too soon,
the mystery that hovered there,
the calls to friends, the friend offput
by my demands for Covid rules;
the day was warm, the light was strong,
but now I fear the romance cools
like dying embers in a pit,
though no one can discover it:
the source of all the human woe
must stay in darkness, safe below.

Nov 21
Tent Revival

A cheery morn in open tent:
the gathering of friendly souls,
the sharing in the waning green,
the walk at night while on the phone...
the puzzle waits, the book is read
the email sent to author's dad
to tell him how much I'd relate
to the wondrous brave young girl he had,
who crossed the continents to find
expression and a longer life...
But here we don't live life divine
and end each day to face more strife
as Covid soars and Trump won't go —

a virus on our politick.
I wish this world weren't filled with woe,
but millions more are getting sick
and no one has the cure just yet.
Though sun for me and tented joy,
while weather's warm and folks turn out
to safely congregate's a ploy
for sliding through these ragged times
beyond the range of churchyard chimes.

Nov 22

Too Many

Cases grow: one million in a week!
The sky is gray, sun refused to peek
and smile down on our sadness as we rake
our leaves, eat outdoors again to take
a breath, imagining a time of health.
We may squeak through, defeat the greed and wealth
determining who lives and dies these days.
As sun goes in and out and virus plays
like shadows on the cave walls of our dream...
Humanity, not working as a team,
is doomed to fail when vaccines come around
if distribution practices aren't sound
and healthcare workers die off while we wait;
let's hope we can avoid the dino's fate.

Nov 23
Did Somebody Finally Say "Ascertainment"?

Our body politic's in rehab
getting through its last DT's,
withdrawing from fake news, denial,
lying, stealing, now to trial,
facing all the mess that's left,
the consequences grave, longterm
neglect and Putin-scotched defenses,
massive death, deadly germ,
crazy cultists waving flags
depicting dictator, and now,
Don's dismantling our spy planes, lags
in certifying votes to plow
through all that's left of institutions
once the envy of the world;
disregarding constitutions,
national and state, unheard
of levels of what once was treason
tolerated by the pols
who fear our despot, as the reason
for their cowardice now tolls.
Their base they bought like coke was spiked.
They all OD'd on Monarch dust.
Unconscious that their deals were miked,
the narcos came as narcos must
and hauled them off to senate prison,
where, unmasked, they cough and wheeze.
I trust the Grand Old Party is on
life support—was that a sneeze?
Did Murphy say to ascertain
election tallies three weeks old?

———————————————————

Or is concession all in vain
if Trumpsters fight in street and bold-
ly hold the power, relapse, cause
another round of misery?
I hope we'll put their show on pause —
get on to healing history.

Nov 24
Blue as Dodgers

The Biden Team trots on the field,
heavy hitters one and all,
but will collective genius yield
results when Trump deflates the ball?
Don plans to be a party, spewing,
Covid-sowing 'til the end,
while pleasing Putin with destruction,
salting fields, still in pretend
mode, a reality show construction
made for TV — will he serve
as some demented host and brew his
plot? Most think Don deserves
to rot in jail, his family too,
while Biden tackles pay-per-view
and liberates the poor, can he
an FDR or LBJ be?
We need big answers, big reforms —
let's pray the Blue Team breaks all norms
and takes those left beyond these tears,
so young survivors thrive for years.

Nov 25
A Visit South for Holiday

Untangling strings of tiny lights,
hanging wreaths, arranging greens,
getting in the spirit while
the Spirit hovers near, unseen.
The veil is thin; the dead are close,
the season wildly mild.
The woods retain some vibrant reds
and yellows; in the sky
the gibbous moon smiles lovingly
upon a quiet town,
where work from home
keeps silent night,
eternal peace, for now...

Nov 26
Floats

They told of rain, but here was sun;
the floats rolled 'neath balloons...
the city smiled, parade went by;
we ate a bit too soon,
but there was light to walk in woods
and movies after that.
Thanksgiving came and went this year
with its layer of new fat.

Nov 27
Sculling With a Green Friend

Sculled down the Anacostia,
biked a bit as well,
ate some more and now to bed,
the weather just as swell
as other days of climate change.
We're melting much too fast...
It's nice right now;
I know, somehow,
it isn't meant to last.
The Trump will leave.
The Trump will die.
The Trump name will be dirt,
but those who live beyond the Trumps
will note that there was hurt,
as many died and more ate less,
lined up to beg for meals.
We'll spend our lives to clean this mess
and pray the planet heals.
Yet selfish ones will ever be
among us to deny
the sharing of the fish and loaves
and one such fiend is I.
Not one small act of charity
do I, now, toward the poor.
Today I see with clarity:
I, too, must do much more.
I'm poor, myself, so give in acts
and writing is one such,
but lacking wit, craft, style and facts,
this won't amount to much...

———————————————————

Nov 28
Covid Creeps Closer

The trip last night,
with whole-moon light,
a belly full of friends and feasts:
so glad I got away to roam
among the liberated beasts
where masks were worn
and distance kept.
I hope and trust we all stay clean...
My dear friend Anne has Covid now,
though "like the flu" — I haven't seen
her since last spring, I miss her, too.
We all must let some visits go.
To travel on Thanksgiving you
and I let down our guard, we know.
We took a risk; the surge comes on,
as many traveled carelessly,
for "Freedom" here must now be won
by tossing off the rules, y'see,
as if the rule to mask and wash
was somehow cramping others' style.
Well, try *that*, folks, and then go mosh
with crowds and spew your hate awhile...
You're digging graves for those you may,
or may not, know, or ever love.
Vaccines are coming — not today.
We've more to lose, and from above
it looks like thinning of the herd...
Forget this "herd immunity"!
There's only one wolf chasing us
and gobbling with impunity

the ones at risk—no matter why,
perhaps they're simply old or poor.
He hunts with one voracious eye;
he doesn't need disguises or
a coat of white in winter to
camouflage him in the snow.
This Covid monster's come for you
and all who watch the Trumpster Show.
Go off with him, your darling boy!
Go lick your wounds and meditate
upon the facts that still will toy
with lies you need to formulate
to salve your wounds and drive you back
to rocks from under whence you came;
it's not intelligence you lack,
but "Freedom" from the hater's shame.

Nov 29
It's Always Something

Now bird flu comes to Europe, where,
despite much better protocols,
they, too, have Covid in their hair,
and now the birds are feathered rolls
of virus that could come to us,
as other bird flus have before...
It's obvious the safest bus
to board is one that gives the tour
of masked lands where the people stay
outdoors and far enough away
from carriers of every kind,
but it's impossible to find

a hidey-hole as Nature fights
Her ailments, such as our fleshed tribe.
The human virus appetites
have hurt Her and she will imbibe
th'elixir that She trusts to keep
herself immune, that is to say,
She'll keep her sharpened scythe to reap
as many as will keep at bay
the wrecking crew that humans are,
enlisting birds and bats and all
Her faithful, summoned near and far...
No matter which weak species fall,
She'll fight to live another day.

Nov 30
Dr. Atlas Exits Stage Right

Full moon obscured by thunderclouds
that break with fury, deluge, booms...
The soggy day was spent in shrouds
with telephones and meeting Zooms.
The news was good, the fools are checked.
Now Atlas, too, has quit the farce;
as Sweden's learned, the herd's neglect
is deadly, there deniers sparse.
Yet here, statistics lie on all
fronts re plague, economy;
we'll never know how bad this fall
was.   As the Trump anomaly
recedes and facts come flooding back,
like rain in global-warming times,
new crises we shall never lack.
So toll the churchbells, *sing* wet chimes!

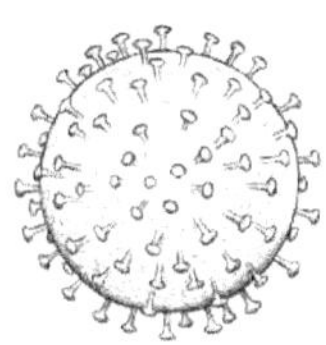

Dec 1
Checking the Headlines

Now "Pardongate" begins with one
big fat redacted document.
We don't yet know who'd paid to un-
do their crimes with Don's consent.
Meanwhile, he floats ideas his kids
should get the pardons they deserve,
in case the heinous things they did
soon come to light as now we swerve
toward Biden. Thus DT brings down
the curtain as he'll torch the place.

Netanyahu goes to town:
assassination new disgrace.
That car, machine-gunned by remote,
held scientist of Iran's nukes.
The Don won't leave a friendly note;
inauguration he rebukes
and plans to launch a new campaign
well-funded by his hoodwinked mobs.
Meanwhile, Congress tries again
to pass relief for rent and jobs.
As Covid soars beyond the Dow,
spent doctors talk of suicide...

There's little that can save this now
sinking ship in rising tide.

Dec 2

Doggerel Wonk

Something's wonky with this day.
Had sudden ton of paperwork
to file for housing office and
a phone gone dead, the new one dropped,
a stick stuck under car that made
a creepy scraping sound, while I
worry always it will die,
(350 thousand miles I've clocked),
steadfast all these eighteen years:
divorce and moves and visits passed,
mileposts on the highway now,
children grown, retirement, loves
live and dead, while 14 books
came through me, though remain unread.
I plan to go with little note...
Then, walking in the cooler air
and talking to my oldest friend,
restored me like a bracing drink;
so now into my bed I sink,
laughing at defecting Barr,
and wishing on a Biden star.

____

Dec 3

About to Get Nipped

A better day, with sun and blooms on
some confused fruit tree I passed
while walking, meditating for
the loved ones suffering afar:
the ones with cancer, broken bones,
R.A., sciatica and more
longterm pain I've still escaped
(it's hard to be upbeat while sore).
The Don is hurting, too, they say,
spinning out and melting down.
Repubs are fleeing day by day
from Trumpworld, though in DC Town
they're planning parties, big ones too:
900 guests to Covid feasts,
ignoring half a million deaths,
evictions, people lining streets
to get a meal or Covid test...
The Biden Team is facing more
healing challenges than this
body politic has faced before.
Now Global Warming's forcing buds
in Christmas Season, where's the snow?
The plagues are coming and the reason
may be that *we* have to go.

Dec 4
Chorus of Chores

Drove a friend to the doc today,
double masked, windows cracked.
Zoomed and chatted: much to say.
Walked with neighbor, only lacked
contact with that special guy,
who takes his weekends to himself.
I swore he'll never see me cry.
I put my heart high on the shelf
and work on Christmas cards instead,
homemade — of course — now piling up
unlike the snow, which falls as rain...
I drink my tea, I rest, I sup.
The days go by; the news is bleak.
The minions suffer everywhere.
My will is strong, my heart is weak.
I stay away from other's air.

Dec 5
Banksy, "Zappa," "Mank"

So sad to see devotees cheer
their naked emperor;
would all these crazies still be here
if Covid was no more?
Must we excuse delusion when
escaping from such death
as boggles even lucid men?
Don swears with every breath:
"I won I won I really won!"

campaigning in the South,
while aiming his old tweety gun
at Dems. His famous potty mouth
elicits roars of vile assent
as empty as the MAGA mind...

Like some of an artistic bent,
in creative thought I find
my comfort, so indulge in three
great docs of artists who
confronted evil-powers-that-be
and to the truth stayed true.
With painting, music, gift of gab,
these greats did more for all
than balding pols, who yell to stab
the righteous as they fall.

I write a poem of my birth
to "luck" and "art" who bore
a golden girl of normal girth
who knew what art was for:
a weapon forged of thought and sweat
to pierce the mail of lies,
something only some may get —
it comes in some disguise...
Today, with Covid, what we need
more than these heads in sand,
is evolution to quick breed
a more resilient brand,
which may be what the Chinese do
as news relates that they
have bred a super warrior, who
is rather hard to slay.

Perhaps the answer will be war
if Covid's not enough;
survival's what we're fighting for,
as global warming's tough.
I turn to genius to console
and hope we thus evolve.
More art would elevate the soul,
improve the pool with love.

Dec 6

Decking Under Solar Winds

I hang my boughs of holly and
ivy on my door.
The weather doesn't smack of snow.
Now Jersey snow seems damned.
The planet reels from warming so,
the birds are all confused;
I sense they're singing courting songs...
how can they all get used
to rhythms never felt before
since man made much of sun,
building temples to adore
the solstice and the one
that now is flaring up again?
She may destroy us quick.
We need our new devices to
keep in touch with all while sick.
I walk in cornfields glorious;
I tell my lancer how
I find the life notorious
for just surviving now.

Now on the news the anchors claim
we've lost our heart to feel
concern for elders everywhere,
who won't have grace to heal,
not to mention children, who
are hungry every hour.
Compassion fatigue's real, my friends;
our love's begun to sour...
We decorate and try to get
some merriment and cheer,
though Christmas will be different for:
it's Covid rules this year.
I listen to Bill Gates explain
how Trump despoiled his plan
to work with China to obtain
new energy for man,
but here we are, no sign ahead
that warming we'll survive.
With sugarplums in hungry heads
we fight to feel alive.
I listen to Bob Dylan ask
when he was young and spry:
"How many ears must one man have
before he can hear people cry?"

Dec 7

For Jocelyn Benson, Rebekah Jones, and
Gretchen Whitmer

As Biden goes on picking competent
heads for his resurrection of the Fed,
the Trumpsters threaten public servants bent

on doing their due diligence instead
of showing abject loyalty to Him,
martyr of the Holy White Cabal.
His chance of re-election growing slim,
each day the Trump team fumbles their own
ball.
For, as my lancer says: "Incompetence
is Don's brand"; we hold out hope that we
will soon draw our due recompense,
replanting Law to save democracy.

Dec 8
"Safe Harbor" Day
(or, "Democracy is Coming to the U.S.A.")

Don's final lawsuits now kaput,
Repubs not willing to admit
he's lost — just say it! *Alles ist gut;*
yet *Verruckt* Donny does not quit.
Meanwhile...in the Biden camp
a raft of new appointees should
please Dem's base and thus revamp
the gummint, making all things good.
Lo! Now my lancer calls me to
complain about Defense Sec choice.
Oh well, I see appeasement there
for black men. But to hear his voice
is so extraordinary that
I couldn't care what rant he's on.

I've walked and mailed out cards and sat
with news shows that expound upon

the great dilemma of our times:
when *will* democracy come back?
Though Leonard Cohen haunts these rhymes,
I fear a new *Dummkopf*'s attack:
another Timothy McVeigh
is armed and waiting for his chance.
And thus, we mustn't look away,
consumed in Biden new romance,
but stick with lover that we've got —
that creaky, old blind lady in
her robes of justice foils their plot,
and gives our system one more win.

Dec 9
As the First Flurries Fall on Fair Princeton...

I shop for my bud whose Covid's on the mend,
address cards, share texts with sexy friend,
listen to the latest Trump-nonsense on the news:
another pointless lawsuit from Ted Cruz.
While vote restrictions mount in bruised peach state,
our chance of dumping Mitch not looking great...

Then on relief bill still stalled:
When I was high-school teaching I might show
a movie that would pose the question: "What
if no Mexicans showed up to work?" and go
into talks of workers' value that
might shake them up a bit, like Bernie, who
insists we fix the aid bill Congress would

pass as tiny bandaid on the blue
state of misery and do what leaders should —
that is, pass a better bill that gives us all
it takes to keep our families afloat.
I stand with Bernie, though I'm sure the call
of Senate roll will yield a different vote.
They simply want to look good for the nonce:
those Grinches all, elitist GOP,
going off to mansions where they flounce
their allegiance to *Das Kapital* decree
that wealth shall always rule o'er poverty.

Dec 10

On Mothers and Reality

On this quiet, sunny Thursday morn,
since leafblowers have left
and ambulances not as yet passed by,
I listen to young mothers bitch and moan:
raising kids in Covid times'
so hard they curse and cry.
I know this would be such a different read
if I were in that stage of life, as I
found married-with-kids without Covid
a trap and then would need
to wail of my domestic woes and sigh
about the children draining me — oh it got bad!
But to be stuck all day with spouse and four
dependents for months with no hope for
relief would have driven *me* completely mad.

"A 9-11 happens every day."

The millions dead in less than one year tell
of deniers still convinced it's gone away,
while drawing their last breath; it won't go well.

Bike by the IAS where genius lives,
where Einstein and his ilk once slaved away,
but now it seems too quiet and it gives
me creeps to think that genius has no sway
upon our ignorant, who wish to die,
rejecting our collective day-to-day
agreed-upon reality that buys
us time to reason things and figure just
how we'll get through this bottleneck...

Perhaps the answer dawning is we must
lose the anti-truthers — what the heck?

At night I try to glimpse the Northern Lights,
which come this low when sunstorms wrack our
orb,
but sadly, though the sky held some delights,
local light pollution would absorb
such delicate designs upon the sky.
I crane my neck awhile demanding "why"?

Dec 11
"A remarkable day in the life of contemporary
America" — Jon Meacham

Just as democracy again was saved,
the FDA approved the new vaccine.
SCOTUS laughed Don's suit into its grave

---

for claiming fraud where no such fraud was
seen.
And now, all hope elixir in the vein
will ward off Covid in the months ahead;
the Trumpsters still won't mask and so insane
big numbers must fill rolls of dead.
I had a pleasant walk in morning frost,
another with a friend this afternoon,
then threw out caution, buoyed that Trump had
lost
(*again!*) and kissed the man I love in our balloon,
or bubble, call it, or call it dumb
luck, we both might get away with this
delight in fireside music that would come
with me on his firm mattress — *bliss!*

Dec 12

A Walk In Upper Bucks

While Proud Boys took to streets in DC just
to wave at Donald as he 'coptered o'er,
I trudged PA's canal path, where, I must
admit, I hadn't trudged before,
photographing red clay cliffs in fog,
and houses old as Washington's HQ
downriver where his army's boats would clog
the icy Delaware once to renew
faith in revolution then thought lost,
'til Trenton Christmas turned the tide around...
I captured in my lens the fearful cost:
a muddied Trump-Pence yardsign run aground
upon a mudflat in the dank canal.

(It must've have blown there on the winds of
change.)

A walk alone might seem a thing banal,
but I find each uncanny, mystic, strange.

Dec 13
Pheasants for Peasants

A bikeride through the local countryside
to see if maybe I could apples buy
at orchard store full of fruit — I tried —
but there were none sold cheaper, right for pie...
Yet ring-necked pheasants danced in nearby field
and people strolled to soak in late-fall sun.
I biked so long my tired legs concealed
a joy I carried 'til the day was done,
anticipating Biden's win *again,*
(for every week he must rewin this race),
as electors vote tomorrow; then,
perhaps at last, Repubs will bravely face
the truth and let us end this tragic year,
cheering Don and fanboys out of here.

Dec 14
Rainy Monday of Electors

300 thousand deaths to date:
that's two a minute — at this rate
we'll see a million dead before

the new vaccines might square the score...
The first injection went today
into the arm of one sweet nurse;
meanwhile, electors had their say:
the fate of Donald even worse.
As loopholes close like coffin lids,
there's plenty mischief yet to do.
I fear his cronies and his kids
will all get pardons 'fore they're through.
I watched the rest of "Leftovers,"
a sci-fi sort of soap about
a rapture with more do-overs
than I could follow, no less tout;
and yet, there were some comic lines
and characters obscuring what
was one more love story divine.
My lancer shows affection, but
will not let down his guard with me,
as our show ends — or we shall see...

Dec 15
Detection of Defection

Like others I must revel in
the death of the Republican:
a Grand Ol' Party once, but now
a cannibal, and Trump cash cow.
To watch it eat its own and die,
delights in ways that even I,
a peacelover afraid of pain,
can see will surely be our gain.
Hey look: we won one! Now Steve Schmidt, of

the Lincoln Project, may not love
the Dems for all they stand for, yet,
he wants to be one now — I get
the feeling he won't be the first;
their situation's growing worse.
The pardons are about to snow
more surely on us now and sow
as much dissent within us as
the cops can take. Though never has
the violence in our streets gone quiet,
there's plenty chance another riot,
or perhaps another bomb,
or church shooting happens on
a day we least expect for we
are focused on democracy
and Georgia's hope for senate power,
which grows as voters spend an hour
or more in line to do their duty...
A senate win would be a beauty!
But let's not get too power-mad;
McConnell's senate, though real bad,
might still decide to pass relief
to gain the day, without a chief
as selfish as a Donald Trump.
It's possible this car could bump
along its normal muddy road,
while remembering to hold
the wheel more steady than to date;
I swear it's not too rough, too late
to right this junker, sally forth
and give the people what they're worth!
Meanwhile, my friend discloses that
she wears an anti-vaxxer hat.

If not a MAGA, she's still gone
around a bend. I feel forlorn,
forsaken, disappointed, though
mere politics aren't meant to throw
a monkeywrench in every bond;
of her I'm still extremely fond.

Dec 16
Snowday!

To celebrate our wonderland of white
I rented "Downhill Racer," '69's
Robert Redford paeon to the sport
as practiced by DS who always said
"It's better than sex" — that crazy dive
down mountains steep enough to kill a bird...
Now I watch the storm alone and think
I am so fortunate to be alive!
The colored lights around my window blink.
My family members seem, so far, to thrive,
and though today I still have not a word
from he who took my downhill racer's place,
the storms today are worse and more absurd
than any time before... Now I will lace
the threads of time to weave the way ahead,
take visions of those blue-green eyes to bed.

Dec 17
Eugenics or Genocide — What's the Crucial Diff?

Before I left to ski around the park,
I heard news unsurprising as it's dark:
emails found can prove once and for all
the Trumpsters wanted millions here to fall
victim to the plague they saw as their
best weapon to kill those they didn't care
to keep around. Blue-Staters, black and brown,
would die along with youngsters; they denied
their own mortality, as they would hide
the truth. The Trump plan: Herd Immunity,
was quickly proven bogus, as it failed
in Sweden. But Trumpsters here prevailed,
systematically, to take apart
the CDC and ravage, to their heart,
scientific bulwarks that should keep
us safe, though lies began to creep
throughout the body politic
ensuring more than should have got real sick.
The National Cathedral tolled today
300 times to send along their way
a thousand times more souls —
more now than fell
in World War II. Americans will tell
survivors of this horrid interlude:
autocracy did none but rich folks good,
for only *they* can get the cure and pay
their way to health. The rest can pass away...

Dec 18
Belly Laughs for Health

The snow's still here;
it must be cold.
I walk the trails and photograph
what seems a disappearing trend:
will winter come again next year?
It's hard to keep up with the news;
this sphere accelerates each day.
The one thing that seems constant is
the notion Trump won't fade away,
nor will this virus, mutating
in England, sure to do so here...
My lancer keeps his silence, his
withdrawal meant to keep me near.
I watch a silly show and laugh;
it feels so right — absurdity
surrounds me like the frozen white
that clothes us to eternity.

Dec 19
Still Overcoming That Stutter

The President-elect can't talk;
he garbles names consistently.
About his choices, who will balk?
His cabinet's persistently
peopled with the colors of
diversity and maybe will
lead us from adversity,
though Trump intends to be a pill

and razz all from the sidelines, though
I wonder who'll be listening.
At noon I skied about in snow
still powdery and glistening!

Dec 20
Relief at Last?

Nine months late and much too light,
Repubs have given up their fight
and so we'll have a small check to
spend for Christmas, help us through,
the calculation, being that,
with Biden in we'll pass the hat
and do a stimulus round two
in time to ward off hunger, flu,
eviction, virus, loan debt, bug,
while still too dangerous to hug.
Moderna says it's rolling out
its own vaccine — without a doubt
the Pence-ster getting his was fine,
the Trumpster says: "Don't give me mine."
He keeps his focus on his coup
and Flynn is one more traitor who
helps fan those flames. The army won't
support this martial law affront.
I ski along a creek and smile;
white stuff lasts a little while,
though solstice may be rainy so
back down my burrow I shall go
without a fire to send the night
around the bend — the lancer might

remember, though I somehow doubt it,
so now expect to do without it...
At least a girlfriend asks me to
eat Christmas dinner with her — whew!

Dec 21
Winter Solstice With "Christmas Star"

Saint Maurice Hilleman smiles down
on Biden baring his arm now
to get the Pfizer flu vaccine;
protection from the clown, somehow,
is what we also hope they mean
to bring us as they clean debris
from White House grounds —
the worst it's seen —
as minions still insist that he
should fire off militia rounds,
declaring martial law, more grave
than undermining plague protection.
We peer through foggy night to see
a special light show new direction:
just Jupiter and Saturn in
celestial spin.   No Jesus here.
In 30 days we'll hope to be
past Trumpland — let these dark skies clear!

Dec 22

Literary Friends Take on the Times

All day I thought about the books
my friends were writing, journeys of
science, spirit, different looks
at how the focus and the love
makes writing clear, concise, of worth.
I never feel my words a trove
of wisdom, let alone of mirth.
Yet, as the new relief bill's passed
and peeps close to the Trumpster say
this stubborn show of force can't last;
it's time to put the guns away
and move ahead to face the facts
that can unite, if only they
are coupled with effective acts.
This plague will never go away
if folks insist it isn't real,
so pass it on and on again.
I am ashamed I can not feel
remorse for such repugnant men
and women who would sacrifice
the future to the present vice
of greed — what else could they be thinking?
Nixon's excuse was he was drinking...
but Don decompensates full bore.
We cannot suffer him much more.

Skies cleared, I walk a little way
and find the "Christmas Star" — hooray!

Dec 23

"$600 is a disgrace — it should be $2,000 a
person!"

The day dawns with hilarity
juxtaposed with tragedy:
now Donny wants to squash the aid
Repubs and Dems had finally made,
after nine long months of fighting.
Seems the totals put in writing
are too little for Big Don;
so hunger, homelessness go on
beneath the freakish "Christmas Star."
We beg the Christchild: "Where you are?"
Oh there are pardons dumped galore
on all Don's cronies — many more
are lined up to be mercy-blessed.
I quiver in my toasty nest
and wonder how we'll squeak through 'til
the 20th — I hope we will...

Dec 24

An Eve with Paul Celan and Eric Idle

"Black milk" they drank
on Christmas Eve,
on New Year's Day,
and every morn.
Black milk is all that's served us now;
the government is broken, torn.
The tyrant's fled to golf in sun.
A doctor dies. A black man's shot.

The System's hacked to pieces by
the Red Bear and now millions got
infected since last holiday,
with millions more about to fall.
The vaccine's hardly wiggled out
of shrouds; the crowds must go without
any form of help this season.
(Selfishness has passed all reason.)
No one really gives a damn
if children spend their Christmas crying.
"No turkey, kids, not even ham."
Still, plenty reckless dopes are flying
through Covid plague-clouds to the winds...
Celan witnessed captives dying
wrote of "Black milk" as of sins.
We're still not in *our* deathcamps, for *our*
Hitler's ineffectual,
but tonight, we'll see more horror...
I sing carols intellectual.

Now, to dispel the darkness,
I know I can rely on
the cheeky Christmas harkness
of Python's *Life of Brian*.

Dec 25
Wind Victims: Just As Vonnegut Predicted

Angry winds disrupt my dreams —
Colorado's here it seems,
but now, with flooding rains as well:
Christmas power-outage Hell.

Up here on Earth we mark in red
our special days. Today the dead
are piling faster than the snows,
the Newsmen's Death-o-meter shows.
"Real People" — and I trust I'm one —
are hurting now and counting on
Feds for handouts. Don says we
real folks deserve a bigger fee.
600 bucks Repubs would give,
but real peeps know they cannot live
on such chump change — so in response,
Trump pockets every bill at once.
Since he can't rule in perpetuity,
he'll deny tax dollars due to you and me.
A Putin tool, he's right as rain:
narcissistic fools feel no pain...
And on this dull Xmas for action,
exploding RV's one distraction.
Let's see if Nashville's perp is one
of Don's fans, or another son
of frustrated, impoverished "Reals" —
a lot of us know how he feels.
Let's blow up shit for Christmas now!
We ain't got presents anyhow.

I dine most pleasantly with two
women friends, who stand true Blue,
and look, as I, toward Biden reign
as if the Christ child's come again.

———————————————

Dec 26
Still Sitting On His Bills

Natch, the Prez did not come through
with life-restoring paychecks that are due
to taxpayers who voted for him and
those who didn't—he can't understand
why he's been dumped, so blows up
government,
much more completely than the guy who went
off the deep end making of RV
a bomb set off in Red Tennessee.
Let's see if he was one of Donald's tribe,
though somehow I don't think that was his vibe.
There's much despair out there to go around,
and Congress, at this point, has not yet found
a way to circumvent the pouting Trump,
so lets economy sink into slump...

I, however, bike out in the sun.
It may be cold and icy, but still fun.
The lancer has removed himself, oh well;
I've plenty friends for comfort and feel swell.
Yet others are too isolated now,
unable to find love and tend to plow
into Covid snow-drifts, dank and dead
as what must be the contents of Don's head...

Dec 27
The Torn and Fraying Truth of it All

More of us are dying every day.
The ICUs are filled up in L.A.
One in seventeen we know about
get Covid now, an undercount no doubt.
The Trumpster waited 'til tonight to sign
the bill that will give something to confine
the misery until the Biden crew
can start the major clean-up they must do...
It seems McConnell must have got to him.
For we all knew, there had been but a slim
chance more than a pittance, this time 'round,
of all potential funding would be found.
When pols decide to find aid for the "real"
people — not the rich who steal
from labor and the ignorant below —
Miss America's torn underpants won't show.

I, for one, stayed happy on this day,
spoke with dear ones near and far away,
collected pinecones for the promised fire
(in case the lancer's true and not a liar).
I must admit, it would be nice to find
a man with heart to match outstanding mind,
but when I have a choice between the two
I choose the mind and end up black and blue...
But not as bad as Nashville's RV guy,
who thinks explosives better way to die —
on *Christmas*, yet, to underscore his pain...
I trust I'll never feel *that* bad again.

Dec 28
Warm Beach Day, Goodall Enough for Me

My good health has annexed me,
forced to grieve for silly things.
"Fake losses, just another swan flown,"
chides this coral-button moon.
Heartbreak must be someplace —
these sculpted dunes?
Maybe if I stare hard enough, the waves...
Much too puppy-playful at this age,
the beach gives me my belated solstice gifts:
a pocketful of blue and green and brown and
white scuffed glass bits,
a plastic triceratops, good as new! It fits
my hand as if a child of two.
Music blasted at the shards of pain,
(self-inflicted, to correct the deficit),
reminds me nothing here is ever done
and I can always come again.
I'm home (too soon) to put away
my sea-gift treasures, lay me down
with Dear Jane and her kids,
whose "Roots and Shoots"
blare horns of hope into Covidtown.

Shamefilled, even a boy's blue
paper sky wrapped in cloud ribbons,
is no place for carefree and contented me,
on this beach of despair:
only gulls,
and a lone piper.

Dec 29
Chez Vous

Beach-moon voodoo worked its charms.
Though I wasn't in your arms,
you fed me and we parsed this year:
our failing nation's pain, the fear —
and then you thanked me for your "rant,"
as anger flows from those who can't
make change where change we must, or fail.
Yet we are not the ones to bail.
We do our bits to help in ways
that ease our minds and pass our days...
I made some origami birds;
you read *Reaganland* and words
of wisdom passed to me.
Back home, I watched that show you said
would move me — yes! I went to bed
with visions of your sugarplums,
as ends the year and new hope comes.

Dec 30
Fuck 2020 and All Its Crimes!

Cold day for sewing, talking, friends...
Kabuki Congress never ends.
The Evil Ones persist in power.
Hungry Ones die by the hour.
I savor munchies from my dear,
who helped me end this shitty year,
when pity fled and all came clear:
the gritty dead won't get a tear,

nor children fed — the cupboard's bare.
The billionaires don't stop to care.
Capitalism must end where
their virus taints the very air
and misery can come to all.
A young Repub was said to fall,
at 41(!), from Covid and
though not a Dem, at least he ran
an honest race, as most would tell.
Tomorrow this year sinks to Hell.
I hope it never more will stink,
but stay anomalous and shrink,
like Don's thin ego in the cold
and Mitch's member, flaccid, old.

Dec 31
One Last Rainy Twenty-four

Tears of Heaven end this year,
at least for for those who live out here.
With global warming at our heel,
the bite of plague now simply feels
like house-cleaning, well overdue.
I trust this rather fickle flu
is only heading a parade
of housecleaners who must invade,
displace the host awhile until
the house is neater, then it will
be more delightful for awhile,
until the next plague shall defile
this human hovel that we keep,
with most inhabitants asleep.

They'll never know what hits them, so
it's a rather painless way to go.
It could be war — we're lucky; that
was once an option that begat
a plague more vicious than this one,
whose work just started. When it's done,
we may see Nature looming large;
remember it's She who's in charge.
Become a bit more humble, or
begin a round of bloody gore,
for battlefields will also serve
to cleanse those who still have the nerve.
Our fat and lazy land won't bite.
Thank gods it's lost the appetite;
besides, the cyberwars are on.
Why spend the trillions neither Don
nor Bernie really want to see
sunk in outdated armory?
A filibuster Bernie will
conduct now on the Senate's hill...
more Kabuki, more delay;
and thus we'll spend this rainy day
dismissing one horrendous year,
and crying our way out of here.

2020 Coda:

I must pause and think on Death,
who keeps us company; my friend
whose father died today, ending his long life
with this long year when *every* day
was tense, sometimes an agony
and time, that noisy tic,

ne'er stopped tocking in our ears...
My own dad looked 'round frantically
for the "24 hour alarm clock"
in his final delirium.
They say Covid comes with hallucinations,
vivid dreams, days of delirious fevers,
crippling aches...they say your sense
of taste and smell are missing,
then displaced, exaggerated, ruined
so that nothing guides your senses.
You remain disoriented, depressed,
neither cured and wholesome,
nor completely debilitated.
You may crawl along for months
with lingering symptoms,
immobilizing despair.
There is no clean break with this demon,
unless one is only half-sick in the first place
and very lucky.
Only the rich can afford the good treatments
in the early stages, when they are effective;
only the rich can get tested whenever necessary
and know where they stand.
Yet the rich can be careless, too,
and a few do die, though not nearly enough.
If only the proportions were inverted —
the rich and brutal dying off,
the poor and meek persisting to old age,
there would be justice,
but justice is gone and may not come back;
it seems to have flown long before we noticed
leaving a primitive landscape
of uneasy beasts.

The herd is thinning, yes,
but the predator new and inscrutable.
There's more fear than with the known
forces of destruction;
the Corona mystery's bigger than
all our little lives put together.
The virus has won, even if it shrinks,
and so will go on shaping us
for the rest of our mortal days.
Bless microbes,
and bless humanity,
in their eternal embrace.

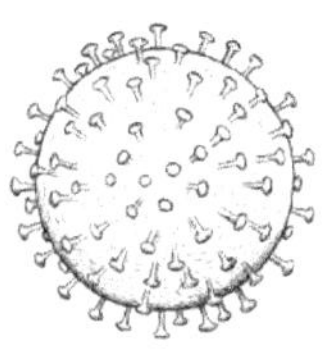

Jan 1, 2021

"In a herd...if you've seen a threat, it's your
responsibility to sound the alarm." —Greta
Thunberg

I shan't pollute this new year with talk of the
Devil;
there's nothing more predictable and void than
evil.
Instead, I hope to grace these last few entries
with homages to the few courageous sentries
who guard our wisdom, hopes and flames for
future
fires 'round which we sit to contemplate and
nurture
solutions to humanity's conundrums. Our
kind's proven
stubbornly to fall prey to this constant coven
of craven capitalists who would see us fail at
being one good, though flawed, species and thus
flail at
rather glaring woes, such as global warming,
as if their ilk can gain from rich folks swarming
off the planet, colonizing Mars because they still
must bend each new environment beneath their
will.

Well, Greta's a Green Angel sailing far to teach
us
that even while the present system cannot reach
us,
we may just squeak through this bottleneck,
avoiding more Titanics as we wreck
upon our methane icebergs, gasping for air.
To sing Ms. Thunberg's praises: only fair,
as I've devoted way too much attention
to the Dark Side, while it lacks invention.
Forward march into the daunting, drifting days
and give the new-hatched heroes their due
praise!

Jan 2
Surely There's a Teeshirt: "I Survived 2020"

I commune with houseplants 'round my place:
Begonia punches out incessant pinks,
Spider Plant, a blossom fine as lace;
Orchid may come through again, she thinks.
Big Fern thrives in light by windowside;
Little Fern I rescued from the woods.
She likes it here enough, but cannot hide
the brown spots on her leaves; none says she
should.
Philodendrons pour from two white pots;
one is climbing up my yellow wall.
Tiny Pine Tree hasn't any knots;
it sits atop the table, cute and small.
Vavilov was tortured, beaten, starved,
defending seeds and science to the end...

____

Outside, I water Ivy, whom I'd carved
from soil in the park, to gain a friend.
Beside her hangs the potted Myrtle who,
may one day greet me on a day of Spring
with blossoms of the purest, brightest blue.
And now, of Vavilov Mom Russia sings,
though once her Georgian dictator denounced
his botanists, who starved in Nazi siege
and never once upon their seed bank pounced
to slake their hunger, for they saw the need
of future humans for their lifelong work,
unlike *our* minions, who would rather kiss
a leader who is nothing but a jerk,
and all the gifts of science gladly miss.
Well, as I've learned a thing or two from plants,
who, needing very little, give so much,
I trust by Wednesday we'll be done this dance,
the nation bloom with wiser, greener touch.

Jan 3

Of My Brother With the Exploding Heart

Today's forever *your* day, absent brother,
who gave me wisdom-faith-love like no other.
I listened to your old recording to
connect with spirit left alive in you.
You wouldn't be so different today,
stout-hearted Irish Catholic as they say,
our president-elect must surely be —
better, even than John Kennedy.
He sure has thrown Dear Leader in a tizzy:
new tape reveals a Loser, very busy

trying to coerce a fellow Gopper
to promulgate another crazy whopper
about election fraud that just ain't there!
I doubt, of this, my Saint, you'd ever care,
as you were bent on music of the spheres
and loved us all, your enemies and dears,
with such a heart well-crafted to explode —
I look for you in Heaven's vast abode.

Jan 4
Chez Moi

Productive day in work and play
rewarded with a visit —
my lancer came, and came,
and it was over-the-top exquisite!

Jan 5
Under Dunkelberger's Bridges

Over the Hudson and through the woods
up the Merritt Parkway drove;
it's always a pleasure to see all the Deco
with workers in bass relief.
Arriving in Mass, I donned my mask
for lunch with a writer-friend.
We walked 'round Northampton
discussing transitions
and hope for a New Age dawn.
Then I snuck into Covid-
controlled Vermont,

hoping I wouldn't get pulled over.
(Heard they exact a transit fine.)
I felt like a smuggler
with my dirty-mob Jersey plates,
which no cop has yet discovered...
The fireplace so cozy,
outside a coyote
prowling in the pines:
what could be sweeter?
Though I hope for a snowfall,
these visits with loved ones here
will take up a few days
dispel Covid bluedays
and bring a Green Mountain of cheer!

Jan 6

Blue Skies, Nothing But Blue Skies...

One dead in Washington;
hope you Proud Boys had your fun.
Hard to tell which side is winning.
Who can stand another inning?
Red-hat monkey swings in Senate,
proud display of rebel pennant,
big guy's feet on Nancy's desk,
crouching Congress, gasmasked mess...
But oh, today, the Georgia wins!
Thus the new Blue reign begins.
I hope this was Trumpshow finale
and no more casualties we'll tally.

Jan 7
Transcending the Coup and Flu

Walked with friend by Deerfield River.
Nature always shall deliver
grace and peace and quietude
to quell the impact of the rude
violent acts of irate men.
I'm hard-pressed to stop watching when
the news is coming fast and grim
and none knows what to do with him—
the devil we can't rid us of,
no matter how much patient love
we open-hearted wish to share
with "victims" who no longer care
that Truth exists, as science does.
We know naught comes of violence, cuz
the revolution has to be
a matter of ecology,
for only when all men evolve
will there be means to problems solve.

Jan 8
More Aftermath of Improbability

A Capitol policeman badly beaten with
fire extinguisher will cease to live,
as well as three more of the nasty mob,
who did, at best, a half-assed hatchet job
upon the big-domed symbol of such liberty
as we pretend to practice, while we sink to be
one more sad, low-class republic where

tyranny accompanies despair.
Speeches, speeches, plenty vowers
to take away the devil's powers...
yet somehow I doubt much will come
of such efforts to remove the dumb
and dumberer from power seats,
as Idiot-in-chief now tweets
he thinks there should be smooth transition.
What makes us think his thugs will listen?
Funniest is watching garbage-
Goppers desperate now to salvage
reputations thin as gruels
they've fed the masses — exit fools!

On a happy note: I shopped
with daughter until we stopped
to cook and dance around her kitchen —
warmish, bright, Vermont is bitchin!

Jan 9
More Deaths from Coup and Flu

Headed home accompanied
by my reporters, whom I need
to feed my head when times are rough...
These choppy seas, my sails gone luff,
but rudder sturdy, holding strong —
(narrated journeys seem less long).
Apparently, impeachment stands
the better chance for changing hands
and fencing out the orange brat,
who plans to run again — eat *that*!

What will ensue in 11 days?
How safely will the Congress haze
in Biden team while crazies plot?
It would be good if someone got
the message that police aren't safe,
and maybe military chafe
at having something fun to do —
protect new Prez? See torch passed through?
I wonder if the army *could*
do better? Gee whiz, *someone* should!

The worst day yet of Covid sees:
the freezer trucks down in LA
so full, they tell the families:
"Put kin on ice, no room to freeze."

And in that Capitol melee
the super-spreader will make sick
those who got out, while some may say:
those Rebels, whose hearts quit that day,
were better blessed to get out quick.

Jan 10
Block and Tackle

A pleasant day to bike in sun,
so grateful to have lived thus far:
our Covid count has way outdone
that of all tribes, where'er they are.

We have arrested some of those
who stormed the DC citadel.

As lawmakers' tempers rose
the censor's ax at long last fell
upon the tyrant's lie machine;
corporates weighed in with might
insisting platforms keep it clean
of violent chat from Rebel right.

It's clear the Biden team will face
a new world of security.
Impeachment fans now grow apace;
removal's not a surety.
We must name names and call them out:
enablers, fascists and their ilk.
At last it's clear, without a doubt,
this coup debacle all will milk,
not least the perps, who plot along...
another coming *Kristillnacht*.
Ol' Schwarznegger sings loud and strong.
We'll hear him, lest his Twitter's blocked...

Jan 11
Self-selective Morbidity

A gray day for a walk with friend
around the schools deserted now;
with students gone, it seems an end
to Princeton as we know it. How
can Biden take on all these woes
while bringing justice, putting down
rebellion, and then, goodness knows,
vaccinating every clown
who still insists the vax is bad?

Will all resistance ever end?
The Rebel-right is merely mad,
no hope their will our courts can bend.
But Covid ought to bring about
a better attitude toward facts;
the healthy remnants need to shout
that staying Covid-free *attracts*.
Who wants to date a maskless joe
who'd just as soon give herpes, AIDS,
as Covid to his girlfriends, who
are likely anti-vaxxer maids?
I hope this slo-mo civil war
will end with Covid helping out
and though 'twill surely leave a scar,
to me, for one, there's little doubt
we needed this sad drama to
draw a redline 'round our ills,
for though it may miss me and you:
sedition, just like Covid, kills!

Jan 12

What, Where, When, Why, Howie

Howard Liebengood was loved by all,
now citizens and congressmen recall:
a man of gentle nature, cookie-sweet,
wore a badge and daily came to greet
those he served and swore he would protect.
I hereby honor him and show respect
for any and all cops who understand
that service is an honor and command
enough restraint to do their duty well.

With loving goodness, Howard's gone to hell.
And here's to Jamie Raskin, who can say
a thing or two of suicide today:
he bravely leads Impeachment Number Two
while suffering a soul sore black and blue
for having lost his brilliant Harvard son...
This course is tough enough, and anyone
too sensitive, too wise to stick it out,
is now excused from class. I also shout
out to the noble manatee who glides
through mangroves, from the harsh sun hides
the shame of having let some yahoo write
"TRUMP" on its back—I hope it thrives despite.
These casualties are three uncalled-for shames
that carry with them more than one bad name,
for all who cling to orange tyrant bear;
the mark of cowardice these three won't wear.
More innocence and goodness sacrificed
to have to rule against this evil *twice*:
point to the minions who may not have died
if Mitch McConnell's senate would have tried
the case a year ago and witness brought
to shine a light; now millions more have caught
the virus, not to mention congressmen,
who crammed into a room for hours when
marauding hordes pissed on our monument
and fellow congressmen would not prevent
the spread of Covid—Gops refused to mask.
For this alone there should be one more task:
to censure or remove the poisoned fruit
who sit in hallowed halls and think it cute
to still play footsie with a president
who tore up their Grand Party to prevent

Romney and the sane ones showing strength;
and now ol' Mitch will go to any length
to exorcise the demon from his brand.
Well, ain't that a little late? The hate's been
fanned,
destruction wrought, terror spread about.
You, McConnell bear the shame — of that no
doubt!

Jan 13

The Yellow Party Wails and Fails

Once more into the breach:
Dems *again* must Don impeach
and now we hear
'twas out of *fear*
those Gops did nothing all these years!
Fear he'd hurt their family,
fear he'd smear them royally —
well, sorry cowards, now you pay.
This was, *again*, your shameful day.
Only ten were brave and true.
And now, Lame Mitch, it's up to you;
and *you* say delay
you say to pray.
Rioters won't go away.
The capital is fortified,
the state houses now boarded up.
I hope you Gops are satisfied;
you've poured your fears into each cup.
You've spread your evil far and wide.
No place for truth-tellers to hide:

we see them bravely speaking now;
the truth will out, the ship somehow
re-right itself and chug along...
but what you've done is evil, wrong
and you must pay by leaving town.
We don't need more Trump dogs around.
You congressmen who would defame
our principals *will* go in shame.
We'll hope the FBI brings light
on how you aided thugs to fight
police, while looking to hang Pence.
There must be *no* legal defense
for you to get away with this!
If you'd a year ago dismissed
the tyrant, think how now we'd be?
Now worms, fear for your family!

Jan 14
Private Idaho Squared

A day to sing the song of self and celebrate
two milestones, mine and one in far LA.
Her husband threw surprise party on Zoom.
To be with them and cats and friends felt great!
At home in virtual reality,
I wonder if I'll ever travel when
so many friends and loved ones I can see
without a farthing, nor a league, I'd spend.
My avatar gives hugs and kisses to
all those who live inside each heart-shaped
square;
the many jokes and memes re Zoom ring true

when everyone is meeting up out there.
Back in the 90's when the gamers sought
to give us worlds to visit, heroes fair,
I, like many Boomers, often fought
our children's keen desire to drag us there...
but now I play along in artifice
where gardens grow despite the lack of sun
and no one knows how we'll adapt to this
brave world where there's a square for everyone.

Back to the news: now Biden tries to bring
a plan to fight the chaos of vaccines;
it seems Repubs had visioned not a thing —
to them the cure was just a fist of beans.
Now if the Dems can get the mission done
and conquer Covid in the coming year,
I wonder if I'll still be having fun
with magic squares that take me there from here.

Jan 15
Things That Go Boom in the Night

I was winding down the day with evening news
when out of nowhere came a mighty boom.
Rattled yes, though to be fearful I refuse,
so peered through blinds around the living
room,
cocked ears for sirens that would surely wail,
or interruption in the live broadcast,
my phone to ring or something that would hail
catastrophe — that test we to failed to pass
to fend off thugs at Capitol before.

And now we're cringing; capitols abound
with boarded windows, beefed up guards
galore...
I couldn't fathom what had made that sound,
but then I heard the raindrops on my vent
and checked the temp — 'twas 45 degrees!
Global warming was the menace meant
to make me start and shake with deep unease.
No, this was no invasion, not a plot
to blow up fed'ral buildings in the name
of some fat tyrant soon to be forgot —
but January thunder — disastrous just the same.

Jan 16
The Duty to Grieve and Believe

My friend's son died suddenly.
Today I went on Zoom to see
her bravely speak with all his friends,
reminder how life quickly ends.
Then watched a show about John Brown,
a picaresque of what's gone down,
as once again we start this fight
to kill the claim that white is might.
I cry and laugh now constantly
in this hour of hilarity
when Earth's lost all stability
as if a grieving family
and John Brown tells us (on this show):
"I am a wealthy man, wealthy in grief"
(a wealth few of *us* could ever know).
"I've buried nine kids and a wife,"

wails Brown. With loss beyond belief
a year ago, in another life,
we couldn't have dreamed how we'd feel
facing all this death and violent strife,
hoping to get through it and to heal
a nation fighting endless civil war,
like many nations scattered 'round this sphere.
A young man's organs live today once more,
(of grief my friend has nothing now to fear);
his death saved lives, a hero to the end.
Her right to mourn I'll steadfastly defend.
As we brace for Biden Day
and celebrate the life of King,
the ending I'll now give away:
John Brown would raise a sword, then swing

Jan 17

Avi Loeb Takes Me Solar-sailing

A day of science, windy, mild:
Loeb says we should save the child
within us to in Nature play
with open minds and disobey
authority's conventions, which
run contrary to learner's bliss
when studying the crazy stuff
of which we haven't learned enough,
like solar sails that argue for
strange planet with cool shit galore,
(much cooler than *our* box of toys),
to whisk through space. The mind enjoys
a glimpse of solar sail from far

horizon of another star...
I walked for hours alone and with
my neighbor friend to whom I give
the inspiration that I find
in such a bursting, fruitful mind,
to seed my dreams and pass like mail
through troubled times, a solar sail,
and marvel that no thugs today
came out with matches, for they play
sick games when they could learn and soar
above their genes and smile much more

Jan 18
A MLK Day Spent the Selfish Way

Biking in unwelcome heat:
The shoots are up; they'll face defeat
when comes the drop. Let's hope they're strong.
I bike and sing my freedom song,
resisting all temptation to
respond to texts from you-know-who.
He wants me and I must obey;
so in his bed I end this day.

I'm grateful I can train my gaze
off politics and plague some days,
for Nature waits most patiently
to see what color bloom will be
emerging from the times of doubt
and cheering hearts both weak and stout.
Some days we live the strength they gave:
the King we'd lose, his words we'd save.

Jan 19
Some Numbers for the Numb

21,000 troops in town
razor-wire rings around.
400,000 dead today.
13,000,000 workers say
they have no work. As Biden goes
down to the Capitol, he knows
the optics aren't too good right now...
Inauguration Eve somehow,
goes on with anthem played above
the ring of Guards, the flag we've loved,
co-opted by the rebels, who
will stand down as DC turns Blue.
As for me, I'd hit the beach
to find a place the news can't reach.
It's all too sad, what we've become.
I, too, feel bad, but won't go numb.
Instead, I pray and give more thanks
we haven't—yet—brought in the tanks,
just trucks to keep dead bodies cool,
while off in Airforce One that fool
will get away to run again.
The GOP will die out when
the Trumpsters steal their votes away.
I hope to live to cheer that day.

And as he gives a prayer tonight
the Biden says: "Turn on the light!"
Four hundred beams shoot upward from
reflecting pool, reminding some
of those who died, most needlessly,
from "Wuham Flu," Don's fantasy.

Jan 20
"Perfect Day" Redux (or "*We* is the New Me")

This day dawns with the Trumpster's flight
from Capital and all who might
convict him if the Mitch says "Yes";
he leaves us an ungodly mess.
The Biden cleanup crew comes in,
another Blue reign to begin.
Let's see how he and Kamala
can resurrect that Camelot
when hopes grew high and folks pitched in,
another science race to win.
Seating experts is a start
and showing citizens his heart,
but let's not kid ourselves that this
will insurrectionists dismiss;
the cruel "Uncivil War" drags on —
it doesn't need a head like Don,
who tells his faithful he'll be back.
We're bracing for the next attack.

Still...

It was a perfect day,
Sun smiled down on DC.
Nowhere would we see
violent acts.
Lady Gaga was great,
so were the fife and drum.
Everyone seemed to come
through with grace.
I watched with teary eyes,
though it was nothing new:
normalcy and what's true
roaring back.
Amanda Gorman read:
symbol of youth today,
young ones spotlight the way
we go forth.
It was a perfect day!
I took a walk with a friend,
talked with loved ones of rend
of red shroud.
Now hear musicians play
to wrap up Joe's first day.
I wish it were every day
and all could always play
wild and free
full and free
glad and free
young and free
brave and free
loved and free
hail and free

as *We*.

END NOTE:
You who have survived to read this now know
well what happened after January 20, 2021…
I decided to end this on a high note, as there
needed to be a terminus to the Trump Regime in
order to restore a modicum of hope to this fair
land. I remain hopeful that, as many millions of
articles and tomes are written on these shocking
and momentous months, this little chip of a book
will float along with all the detritus of our times,
perhaps to be plucked from the sand by some
scholarly beach-comber who seeks yet another
obscure point of view. Hope is not as wind-
tossed as she sometimes seems — I think she's an
albatross. Thrive, good readers, thrive!